I0830035

THE BLANK PAGE
A GUIDE TO ORGANIZED WRITING

Dr. Gerald L. Kovacich

authorHOUSE®

AuthorHouse™
1663 Liberty Drive
Bloomington, IN 47403
www.authorhouse.com
Phone: 1 (800) 839-8640

© 2019 Dr. Gerald L. Kovacich. All rights reserved.

*No part of this book may be reproduced, stored in a retrieval system, or
transmitted by any means without the written permission of the authors.*

Published by AuthorHouse 01/23/2020

ISBN: 978-1-7283-3648-0 (sc)
ISBN: 978-1-7283-3647-3 (hc)
ISBN: 978-1-7283-3646-6 (e)

Print information available on the last page.

*Any people depicted in stock imagery provided by Getty Images are models,
and such images are being used for illustrative purposes only.
Certain stock imagery © Getty Images.*

This book is printed on acid-free paper.

*Because of the dynamic nature of the Internet, any web addresses or links contained in
this book may have changed since publication and may no longer be valid. The views
expressed in this work are solely those of the author and do not necessarily reflect the
views of the publisher, and the publisher hereby disclaims any responsibility for them.*

CONTENTS

DEDICATION

This book is dedicated to those who sacrifice their time to become a writer; who fail and still try again, who fail yet again and still try again, always striving to write what is in their mind and in their heart; sharing their ideas, their thoughts, hoping that someone will someday enjoy reading them.

ACKNOWLEDGMENTS

Thanks once again to my great friend and editor for over 21 years, Sandy Nichol. She has always been as reliable as the sun rising and setting. She continues to remind me about working with editors: don't contradict them and don't piss them off.

As always, I acknowledge my friend, Deanna E. Richards, who leaves me alone to write—well, most of the time.

A very special thanks to my friend and talented artist, Meg Mason who is always available to provide art work for consideration for my book covers or other locations in my books.

I continue to appreciate the friendship of my fellow authors and past co-authors. A special thanks to Dr. Vicki L. Anensen-McNealley, Bill Boni, Ed Halibozek, and Dr. Andy Jones, for their contributions to this book. They've all co-authored books with me. Also thanks to Dr. Andrew Blyth and Perry Luzwick for also co-authoring books with me in the past.

Thanks also to those at AuthorHouse who supported me on this book project as expertly as they have the others.

WRITERS' QUOTES

Advice to young writers who want to get ahead without any annoying delays: don't write about Man, write about a man.

E. B. White

To live my dream, that is to be a writer, makes me glad, but never happy: each new book is a challenge, and diving in your soul is not always a good experience. Nevertheless, this is what I chose for me, and I find joy in a Good Fight.

Paulo Coelho

You are not writing for the cause, for humanity, for posterity. You are writing because you want to write; and if you do not want to, you do not have to, neither today, not ever. Remind yourself that it is all for your own happiness, and if you truly dislike the activity, do not try it. Writing is too difficult to do with a half-intention.

Ayn Rand

OTHER WRITER'S COMMENTS

Over the years, I've written books with friends. Four of them share their views recalling writing their first book.

Dr. Vicki L. Anensen-McNealley: The notion of writing a book was initially a romantic one – I envisioned myself pouring incredible ideas onto the page without interruption, with a seemingly effortless completion of thought.

And then I started to write with several book ideas on my mind, I'd discover times when I wanted to write in one book and not another, or focus wholeheartedly on one topic alone and find it difficult to move to another topic, another chapter. My regular day job interrupted my writing, and there have been days…weeks even…where I've not written a sentence.

Deadlines loomed without inspiration, resulting in what felt like forced words on the computer screen. Deleting and rewriting became the norm, until the whispers of my mentor in my brain saying something like, "Just get it down and move on. You can edit it later." Those wise directions led to a flood of ideas and allowed me to toss aside the worries of day-to-day life and reconnect with my passion.

I find myself sneaking away from my "real" life—early in the morning with a hot cup of coffee, before the sun and my family have risen, or late at night when only the clock seems to be moving – to write. I write best in a dark quiet room, with candles and incense burning and my mind racing, aching to get thoughts on paper. My family has come to know these times as MY times – don't interrupt, do not disturb times. I enter the room with energy and fire in my belly, and later escape, exhausted but [usually] satisfied with the results.

Those are my favorite aspects of writing. My least favorite is the editing process. It seems that one cannot edit enough, and certainly cannot maintain the level of enthusiasm initially reveled on the given topic. The book and its chapters become hated in a way, as if you've overindulged on a specific food so much that you'd be fine to never eat it again. It's as if you've lost your shine, and ache for the book to at last reach its final form so that you can finally move to the next book, the next idea – one that is fresh and interesting and grabs your attention once again.

Vicki has just completed her first published book.

Bill Boni: Many people believe they have something worth sharing with the world, and some elect to share through writing and publishing a book.

My first book, I was lucky enough to team up with an experienced writer who guided me through the many pitfalls and perils of publishing. Not everyone is so fortunate, but I believe it really helps to have a personal "sherpa guide" who can help you achieve your own personal "Mt. Everest" moment of achievement!

The process was a lot more involved and required significantly more dedication, discipline and focus than I imagined when I blithely described to prospective publishers what we planned to say and how we'd approach our topic. Since I had already done a number of public presentations to various professional associations and conferences on the general topic of the book, I believed little more would be involved than pulling out the power point slides and capturing my "talking points" used when making the public presentations.

However, the actual process involved finding and recording appropriate footnotes/citations and then physically typing out the dialogue which was the foundation of each chapter. Since the book had to be standalone and I was unable to react/respond to readers the same way I did to live audiences, much more thought was required to provide context and support my assertions. I also learned that my typing speed (as I was doing this way back in the 20th century!) was not adequate to sustain fast production of drafts. Likewise, the tedious process of editing and refining drafts into copyeditor ready versions took longer than expected.

All this was completed over a period of many months and a final heroic long weekend of non-stop revisions. The result was a suitably prepared draft that went for professional editing by the publisher. After several rounds of modifications and revisions it was finally "done".

There are few more satisfying moments in life than when we can see the results of the hard work required to create a tangible product. That first book, as delivered from the publisher, still sits on my bookshelf. Nearly 20 years on from that time, It remains one of my proudest achievements and provided many additional professional and personal benefits that continue to the present.

Bill Boni is now the author of three books, to include one translated into Japanese.

Ed Halibozek: The idea of writing a book is both inspirational and intimidating. I believe many people think about writing a book but very few actually do. I was in this category until a friend suggested to me that we collaborate together, writing a book on corporate security. Since we were both security professionals at the time, the idea intrigued me and it did not take long for me to agree.

At first, I struggled with starting the writing process. Staring at a blank piece of paper is intimidating and non-productive. But, after discussing my approach (or lack of) with my co-author and writing mentor I was able to get started.

I realized I needed to approach writing like a job. Even thought my free time was limited, as I was already fully employed, I needed to allow a specified amount of time each week for writing. I also needed to develop a schedule. One that encompassed the time it would take and the necessary steps, tasks, and actions that needed to be completed from start to finish. And then, the challenge was staying on schedule. I quickly realized that getting behind schedule was easy. Staying on track required discipline and a commitment to the project and to my co-author in order to stay on track.

With all of this sorted out, I found the best approach for me was to start with an outline of the entire book and then work to fill in details. I also learned the importance of writing down all of my ideas (quantity) and worrying about editing (quality) them later. My co-author and I would periodic share what we wrote with each other in order to ensure our writing was consistent in style and content. As we approached the end of our effort, we got together and went through the entire book, page by page, as a final edit. The process worked. This experience of co-authoring a book enabled me to write additional books and to help a new co-author successfully understand what it takes successfully write and have a book published.

Ed is now the author or co-author of 12 books including second editions and one translated into Chinese.

Dr. Andy Jones: When I agreed to write my first book, the first thought was that this was a daunting prospect and there was a massive amount of potential material to cover. I was lucky in that I had a great mentor who had already authored a number of books, so I was guided through what we needed to do and a process for how to do it. The main issue that I had to address was that of time allocation for the writing. I had a full time job that involved a significant amount of travel and making sure that I allocated useful time to the research and writing was a discipline that had to be developed. The second issue was that of working with a co-author and making sure that the writing styles were compatible to ensure that the book we produced read well. It was a steep learning curve but very rewarding.

Andy is now the author and co-author of seven published books and working on a second edition of one of them.

PREFACE

I've been a writer all my life, from love letters to girlfriends, protest letters to corporations and government agencies, articles for national and international newspapers and magazines, a monthly column in the Elsevier cyber security journal for four years, and various other forms of writings. I always thought someday when I had time, I'd write some books, fiction and non-fiction. However, there never seemed to be enough time to write that first book. After all, work and family always came first.

Then, as I was nearing retirement and had a publisher friend who wanted me to write for her publishing house, I decided in 1996 to get to it. After thinking about it for far too long, I reached a point in my life when I decided it was time to put up or shut up. So, I got serious about it. In the last 23 years of writing over 20 books for four publishers as a co-author with trusted friends, mentoring those who wanted help writing their first book, and as the sole author, I learned a few things as I developed a process of writing. My process, learned over time, has been successfully used by me, my co-authors and those who I have mentored. This book is based on that successful process.

The information provided in this book is based on my experience and my opinion on the matters discussed. You may or may not agree with some of it but I offer it as a starting point in your quest to publish your first and subsequent books.

I hope that it will help you more effectively, efficiently, and successfully write your first book and other books to follow. I wish you much success.

INTRODUCTION

The idea for this book started many years ago when I began mentoring people who wanted to write a book or books. They wanted to be a "writer"; a writer of books. So, this book is focused on the process of writing books but it can apply to writing magazine or journal articles and even preparing lectures.

It sounds cool, "I'm a writer." When you tell people that, they usually are interested in knowing more about you, and your writing. There are many reasons why someone wants to be a writer. Some want to be a writer as an ego trip—be acknowledged as a successful writer. Some want to write a story about their life for their family or because they think they have interesting life experiences that others would want to read. It seems most of these "my life" books are really not interesting unless you are very famous, infamous, or your life is truly unique.

Some may want to be fully employed as a writer or as a part-time job. Others may want to write as a hobby. Maybe it relaxes them, gives them a chance—a reason to hide-out from family, and friends once in a while. You can tell your family and friends that you have to go to your office and close the door as you need quiet and privacy to write your book. That excuse may work for a year or more but eventually they'll find out when you don't produce a manuscript. On the extreme end, it may even cause a split-up of marriage or partnership—your partner may think, maybe for good reason that you just wanted to avoid them and used writing as an excuse, as one extreme. To be a true writer requires quiet, privacy. In other words, to be isolated from other human beings. This alone, may stress relationships to the breaking point.

Hopefully, when you began to read this book, you didn't pass over the quotes stated in the front of the book. Yes, there are many people who want to be a writer. I like Ayn Rand's quote. She explains it very well (See Writer's Quotes).

> *Writing is a lonely profession. It is not something that you generally do with others. However, there are of course exceptions like when you agree to co-author a book. Even then, you usually write alone on agreed upon divisions as to who writes what parts.*

Before or after your book is completed, you'll seek a publisher. For your first book, I suggest writing it first because then there is no pressure to hurriedly finish it because you have a deadline to meet. Writing should always be enjoyable. Hurrying to meet a contract deadline for your publisher will probably not be enjoyable.

You may send your book proposal or complete manuscript—using each publishers's specific online guidance to over 100 publishers with potentially all saying no thanks or you may not hear from them at all.

In today's publishing world, I recommend you fill out each publisher's online book proposal form and do not send them the manuscript of your finished book. There are various reasons for this including they probably won't read it but just look at your book proposal. The manuscript may not be as complete as it could be and it gives them a chance to glance at it and reject it out-of-hand.

You just dedicated more than a year of your life or at least your spare time to the project and it has all been a "waste". Being a writer means isolation and being able to face blunt criticisms and outright rejections. Research the life of some famous writers and you will probably find that they were often rejected. Perseverance, probably some luck, or your Karma may make the difference—plus a good story of course.

When most people find out that I am a writer, they ask about it and then say they also want to write a book. One wanted to write about his life in prison. Funny thing is that unless you are famous, infamous or have a very interesting life, no one really wants to read about your life—my opinion. Others wanted to write about their lives for their families, e.g. a family history. Those would be for family eyes only. Even so, you want it to be a professional job without errors of any kind.

When someone asks for advice or some sort of help in writing, I always test their resolve by giving them a series of writing-related tasks and tell them I would meet them in a week and they must bring with them their assigned and completed writing assignment. The vast majority I never see again. Those very few who have done their assigned homework I sometimes mentor. The other, usually want to go it alone. I sometimes wonder how many of them actually finish their book. It's maybe like those working on a PhD. As I understand it, the majority of them never finish their dissertation. In other words, "all but dissertation" (ABD).

I've run across a few people who tell me their idea for a story and then say since I'm a writer, I should take their idea, write the story based on their idea and they would split the royalties with me. Really? Wow, they sure did the hard part. Now all I would have to do is write something on each of those 125–350 or so blank pages. Nothing to it, right?

As a writer, you'll meet all kinds of people who want to be writers. Maybe, I think most, will never write that book. It's like wishing they will win the Lotto. If you don't buy a ticket, you'll never win.

This book is not as much about how to write your book but mostly about a method, a process, for an organized approach to writing your first and future books. It also discusses the current publishing environment. This is important to know as it is obviously the world that you will be in as a writer and one that will always impact your writings.

I wish you luck in your goal of becoming a writer—a true writer with your first published book.

CHAPTER 1

A LOOK BACK FORWARD

I think most people don't appreciate the art of writing, especially in today's world. We humans apparently started out drawing on cave walls and the various symbols eventually were developed over the centuries.

For our purposes, we'll be looking at the English language; however, the same basic human approach to writing applies to all languages.

We went from the pictorial symbols on caves as a means of communicating, to our present form of symbols. When you look at the 26 letters of the English language alphabet, they are in fact a sort of pictorial means of communication.

We take these symbols we call letters and mix them in various ways to form words. These words are then combined to form sentences. These sentences are combined to form paragraphs, pages and into books. The writers use this vehicle to get their thoughts from the brain to some physical or digital form to tell a story and share the thoughts that are in the their heads.

We went from cave markings, writing on bones, wood, papyrus, paper, and now digital form. Our tools are constantly changing. We've gone from a quill, ink and paper to typewriters, often with carbon paper so we can have multiple copies. Then we progressed to the printing press to copy machines. Now we have computers, computer networks and the mother of all communications, the Internet with all its social media and blogs.

Do you remember the time when computers were suppose to make us a "paperless" society? Instead, because of computers and cheap printers—not including those expensive ink cartridges—we pour out more paper than probably ever before, and more books because it is now easier and cheaper to do, especially with the ever-expanding self-publishing business.

It's a great time to be a writer. You can touch symbols—letters—on your computer keyboard, make the words, sentences, paragraphs, so on and so forth that can be understood by our fellow human beings who are educated in the same language we are using. Here is the really cool part: we can now put it in an electronic address in email, push the send button and send it to anyone on earth (who of course have email, txt or such) and in the blink of an eye be received. In doing so, one or millions of people will know what we are thinking. I think that isn't appreciated these days and taken for granted. Regardless, I think that's awesome!

SUMMARY

The art of communication has changed over the centuries. It is easier than ever to exchange ideas in nano-seconds around the world. The advances in technologies have made being a writer through technological support tools much easier, and yet more competitive.

CHAPTER 2

BEFORE YOU BEGIN

Before you decide to give writing a try, ask yourself this question: Why? Why do I want to do this? Is it for fun? To feed my ego? Enjoy writing as a hobby? Fortune and glory? Something really worth sharing with others? For additional or full-time income? These are important questions because how you answer should be your main driving force for writing. There will be many days when you will probably want to give up, take a break (but maybe never start again), have writer's block, or find other things that occupy your time that are not as difficult, as demanding, or others maybe more demanding like family.

For whatever reason you choose to be a writer of books, it will be your main focus: the goal, the objective. No matter what you call it, it should be disciplined enough to push you, drag you, pull you forward until your book is completed and published. It should occupy your mind, sometimes even keep you awake at night.

If you know why you want to write then ask yourself, do you have the mental capability, discipline, time, and language skills to write? Of course you should be objective about it.

If not sure, maybe first write a short story, run it through your software's spelling and grammar checker. Be sure your spelling checker actually corrects the words you want to use and not replace them with the correct spelling of some other words that doesn't make sense in the context in which you want to use. it. Then, if you trust your family members or friends to be honest with you, ask them to read that short story and tell you what they think of it. Remember, your family and friends may be polite and not want to hurt your feelings. So, keep that in mind too. Watch their expressions as they read. That may give you a clue as to their true feelings about what you wrote.

> *I recall the movie "Funny Farm" where a guy quit work to write a novel, and when done, gave it to his wife to read as he sat in a chair watching her in anticipation of a glowing report. She gave him a very negative review. He got mad and threw the manuscript in the fireplace. So be careful what you wish for as you may not get the results you desire. However, that should be taken as a sign to re-write, start another book or consider not being a writer.*

If you've already made up your mind, then by all means charge ahead—but wait. Should you in parallel or before taking on that book, take some writing classes? There are some who will tell you that you indeed should take writing classes, maybe even get a college degree in writing.

I'll give you my philosophy on that. I don't believe in taking writing classes unless you are not confident in your own abilities to string thoughts into sentences, paragraphs, and pages concluding in a book. Then maybe, you may want to try formal classes. As a substitute, you may want to read books about writing, how to write fiction, non-fiction. How to write dialogue, develop characters, evolve a story. There are pros and cons to each.

If you decide to take a writing course, research your teachers. You may find they teach writing but have never had a book published by a publishing house without having to pay for that publication, e.g. it was a self-published book. There is nothing wrong with that and I personally like that approach to self-publication but that's for a subsequent chapter. Maybe they teach it because they can't write a book acceptable to a publisher.

Let's take a baseball batting coach as an example. They can show you how to stand in relation to the plate, how to hold the bat, raise your arms, and all that. However, you still have to correctly swing the bat and safely hit the ball. Another great example is golf lessons. You can learn from an instructor, or videos, but you still have to correctly swing the club. If not, you'll be hooking, slicing, or your ball will fly in some other horrible trajectory. Unfortunately, I can personally attest to that.

Is there a right way to write? Some secret formula? For some, yes, but for a new book writer probably not yet.

> *I believe we are all unique human beings having unique backgrounds, education, and experiences. Therefore, we are unique writers and that being the case, write it your way.*

If you followed the "tried and true" way of writing that some teachers may want you to write, you may miss that unique writing style that is all yours. The concern may be that if all potential book writers took some basic writing class, they and their fellow students may try to be writing in the same, taught style. Look at today's and yesterday's successful writers. They all have their unique style and generally in their chosen genre.

I've heard from those who have taken a writing class or two that they get writing assignments, a short story for example, and then during the next class, they read it aloud in class and not only critiqued by the teacher but by the entire class. What? Your fellow students are there to learn how to write and they are critiquing your story? Based on what? As a fellow writer? Hardly. As a reader or listener? Maybe.

As for me, I only need one critique and that is from my publisher or potential publisher. If your manuscript is accepted, you will be assigned an editor to read it, request you make changes and such. They are the only ones you need to get acceptance from because if you do, it means a book contract and the publication of your book. The publishers and their editors have years of experience and know what will sell. It's kind of a Yin-Yang thing—keep things in balance: their advice and the integrity of your work.

They say a writer is also a reader and yes, that's true for most of us. Now when you read as a writer, don't just read the story. Analyze the style, how the words are put together and look at how the dialogue is done. Also get a sense of how the story flows. A word of caution here. Do not copy anyone's style. Do it your way and do not copy others. Seems like a contradiction but as you do it, it should find that the two compliment each other—reading for enjoyment and also analyzing the author's flow of the story, the words used, and the author's basic writing techniques. Also the "Catch-22" is that when you spend time reading, you are not spending time writing. I often think, "Why am I reading? I should be spending those reading hours writing."

Speaking of copying, if you like a certain author, you probably read whatever books that author has written. After a while and, I believe in many cases of successful writers, you will see a writing pattern and why not? It worked the first time, the book sold well. Therefore, the author will use that basic formula and just plug in variables. Of course that's not as easy as it sounds but in many cases, you'll recognize it. Write in your own style. Make it uniquely yours.

SUMMARY

Before you begin that first book, you should examine what it takes to be a writer. There are pros and cons. Being a writer sounds great but it requires sacrifices by you, your family and friends. Do an objective self-analyses of your time, relationships and environment. If you believe you can take on the job of a writer, by all means, do it. However, as a writer, use your unique style and don't try to copy the styles of others.

CHAPTER 3

PROJECT PLANNING YOUR WAY TO A PUBLISHED BOOK

There are various methods of writing and getting your book published. You must find the best one that works for you. I advise you not to just start writing. In management terms, your writing process should be effective and efficient. What that means is getting the book from your head to your publisher and you're focused on accomplishing that goal with the least amount of wasted time and effort possible. This is especially true if you are writing part-time and have a full-time job. Thus, develop a project plan in at least an outline form if not in detailed form.

I use the philosophy: "When I go slow, I go faster". What I mean is lay the foundation first—get organized and then follow that roadmap.

The first thing to do is to come up with a name for your project. It could be as simple as "My First Book". I prefer the title of the project to be the draft title of your book. I say draft title because your story may take you in a surprisingly different direction making your draft title obsolete. If you have several books in your head that you are going to write, then each book should have a separate project plan.

> *My co-author and I wrote a book which started out with the title "Alzheimer's Curse: Dealing with Your Loved One's Deadly Disease". The final book title is:"The Alzheimer's Plan: Caring for a Family Member". Another benefit of a great editor. Mine once again came through with a better title. I wrote a book called "Poems of Love" which my editor changed to "Essence of Her". Once again a better title—at least in my opinion and hers.*

Once you name your project, then write in one sentence the objective of this project such as "OBJECTIVE: Write this book and have it published by December 12, 2021". What this does is starts to get you focused on writing the book. You may want to call it the "GOAL". It doesn't matter to anyone but you what you call it. It just states in simple terms what you want to achieve using this writing project plan approach.

The next step is to write down all the significant milestones and tasks that are necessary for you to accomplish your objective. Milestone example:

- Establish a place to write
- Set-up document and support storage
- Company name as a writer?
- Company web page as a writer?
- Create a separate email and text identity?
- Establish a writing template
- Establish your research process
- Establish writing progress goals
- Begin writing
- Finish writing first draft
- Edit and re-write - 1x
- Edit and re-write - 2x
- Edit and re-write - 3x
- Edit and re-write - until you are satisfied it is your best effort
- Submit to your editor
- Re-write based on editor's requirements
- Research potential publishers

- Complete the proposal format of your potential publisher
- Submit your proposal to your potential publisher

Of course your specific plan should be one that meets your objective, those of your potential publisher, and writing process in more detail. The above is just a generic example of possible milestones.

> *I suggest you read this entire book before finalizing your book writing project plan because some of your milestones should include meeting the specific demands of your publisher's proposal format; as well as other parts of the publication process required by your publisher.*

In my process of writing a book, I found that I must do at least six edits and re-writes before I'm satisfied it is the best writing of the book that I could have done. However, your chances of missing something is still possible, even probable. Thus the need for a professional editor. I can't over-emphasize that need. It's worth the cost, especially if you are going to self-publish. The last thing you want is to have your book published with spelling and grammatical errors. Imagine the embarrassment, which makes you look like an amateur and not a professional writer who should be taken seriously. On occasion, I find books that are self-published that way. Remember that old saying: "If you go cheap, you get cheap". At the same time, the chances of some error in your published book is always possible since written by humans and edited by humans. Obviously being human, we make mistakes. This book is probably no exception.

> *There are project plan software applications you can buy or maybe find a free one. If free, run it through a malware checker. Most of those I found were too formal and restrictive for my needs. A spreadsheet works fine for me.*

After you have identified your milestones, then under each milestone should be a list of tasks to be accomplished in order to meet each milestone. Each task should also have a due date. So, when your project plan is written, you have your objective supported by milestones and each milestone supported by tasks to be completed in order to meet each specific milestone. It is a typical, basic project plan tailored to writing a book.

For example, in order to accomplish the milestone of "Establish a writing template" some tasks may include:

- Identify at least three published books of the genre that is similar to your book
- Identify their books' formats
- Determine the format you want to use or use the book template cited in this book
- Set up a word processing template using that format
- Make a copy of that template and file it for future use for writing other books
- Rename a copy of that template the working title of your book (the title may change based on your editor or your preference when the book is completed but the working title is useful for establishing your filing system in both hardcopies and digital formats)
- To differentiate between versions of your draft manuscript, you may want to add a number as part of the file name or add the date you last wrote and edited it.

Another thing to do before writing, is to add realistic dates to each task and each milestone and finally to the Goal: "Write this book and have it published by July 1, 2023". These dates are themselves goals and subject to change based on events that you cannot foresee. However, they are great as they give you something to strive for each and every day that you write.

How do you establish these dates? Logically start at the beginning with your completion date objective and please be realistic. In doing so, you won't have to be continuously changing dates. In order to set dates you need to establish a writing time, dates to write, e.g. 8pm-12pm, Monday-Friday. There are of course things to factor in such as appointments, time with friends and family if need be. So, set your dates and then consider doubling the time necessary to complete each task. That is realistic and helps eliminate some, but not all, of your interruptions which may also include deciding to restructure your story, writer's block and such.

You can start with the end date and work backwards or start with your first day of sitting down and getting started on your writing project and work forwards to determine your completion date. If your proposal has been accepted and you are under contract with a specific manuscript delivery date, you already have a date to be completed. Therefore, you'll be working backward to your first day of writing. Hopefully, you would have properly planned or you may find that you'll have to compress some of your writing schedule to meet the contract delivery date. Therefore, and especially with your first book, I recommend you have your manuscript done in at least first draft before contacting a publisher.

> *I never had writer's block—at least so far. I will stare at the computer screen sometimes for hours but I will write something in that book each writing day come hell or high water as the saying goes. I may read it later and delete all of it but that is still progress as you found out what not to use in your book. You may want to consider writer's block as part of your scheduled tasks, milestones and delivery dates. I don't.*

I recommend that you set a specific writing time each day that you write and in your writing place. Writing is "work" so treat it that way. Be disciplined. There will probably be days when you can write five good pages and days when you're lucky to write one, but keep at it. Grind it out, and make progress each and every writing day. Forward, always forward to meeting your objective. As part of your writing research, you may find it interesting to read books about writing by successful writers. You can read when they write, their processes, where they write, etc.

A word of caution: develop your own writing hours, writing environment. What works for them may not work for you. Be an independent thinker and writer. Do it in a way that is comfortable for you. Imitating other writers usually doesn't work except by coincidence. I have found that some of the BookTV interviews delve into the interviewee's writing hours, where and may even show photos of their writing place which is never in a family or public area. It may happen but I haven't seen it during interviews of writers. As a writer, I find the life and writing routines of other writers interesting; however, I would never try to copy their routine. Each of us must write in our own way and in our own time. If not, you'll find yourself fighting that routine because it is not natural for you.

SUMMARY

Establishing a project plan for writing your book will help you get and stay focused. It will allow you to set up writing times, and set realistic milestones, tasks in a more effective and efficient manner. If you have a family, then that schedule will let them know when you are and are not available.

CHAPTER 4

WHERE TO WRITE BEFORE YOU BEGIN TO WRITE

Before you begin to write, you should find a place conducive to writing. Some people may be able to write in the living room while others are watching television. I'm not sure any serious writer can do that but you may be one of them. You may be able to write in the kitchen while your significant other is fixing a meal. If so, more power to you.

The vast majority of us, I believe, need an isolated and quiet spot conducive to thinking because after all, thinking is the first step in the actual writing process. Ever hear someone complain, "I can't hear myself think?" As a writer, you must be able to hear yourself think.

Now that you have decided to be a writer, no matter if full-time or part-time or when you can as a hobby, ask yourself, "Where can I go to write in peace and quiet, and not be disturbed?" If you have a spare room, that would be great, or maybe a desk in the bedroom? If you live alone, then you control your home environment and isolation, quiet, are generally not issues you must deal with. You may like to write with some genre of music playing or maybe you need complete silence. The key is to establish a writing environment that works for you.

The bottom line is that you need a place to spread out research material, file research material, place your printer, store paper, cartridges for your printer, etc. A place where none of that will be disturbed. Yes, I'm speaking of the best physical environment conducive to writing.

What happens if you don't have any such place? If you don't, then what do you do? Where do you go? If you're lucky enough to have a library nearby, maybe take your laptop there. If you have a desktop computer, then maybe you'll have to get a laptop? At libraries, you also have wi-fi, so doing research online won't be a problem, and you also have the library of books to draw from for your research.

> *What is the ideal writing place? That's up to you of course but in summary: a place where you can close the door and have peace and quiet, and not be disturbed. A place where you can have a filling cabinet and other storage space. Wi-fi connection is of course pretty much a necessity these days for research and other forms of communication with anyone supporting your bookwriting project.*

What else do you need to establish for your writing environment? If you have a family in your home, or a partner, you should get their support. If not, and they don't support you by at least leaving you alone when it is writing time, it's another difficulty you must somehow overcome.

If you want to be a writer, really want to be a writer, you'll find a solution. It may be as drastic as taking over part of the garage and remodeling it into a writer's studio or telling the kids your evicting one of them, cramming them into bunk beds and using one of their bedrooms as a writer's studio. Of course, your relationship with the family may suffer but that often happens anyway when you isolate yourself from others for hours a day, maybe all day and night.

> *Being a writer is a lonely profession and sacrifices must be made. Therefore, don't take writing as some frivolous endeavor. Being a writer is serious work and should be treated that way.; however, it should also be fun.*

SUMMARY

Establish a writing environment that will allow you to go and focus on writing without being disturbed by noise, and people. A place where you can set up files, research material, storage space. A place where you can cut out the outside world and focus on writing and hang a "Do Not Disturb" sign on the door.

CHAPTER 5

WRITING TOOLS AND TECHNIQUES

What are the tools of the writing trade? Let's start with the obvious: a good word processing computer. You may have one that is ready to use. It can of course be a laptop, or desktop. If possible, it should be one dedicated to your writing business. A family computer used by others will obviously cause issues as far as the time when the computer is available and keeping your research and writing separate from others who use the computer—"Sorry dad, I didn't mean to delete your files."

A desktop obviously limits where you can write whereas a laptop can be taken on business or other trips, vacations, etc. So, it offers more flexibility and helps to support your project plan writing schedule. What size screen should you have? A 17" screen is great. After many hours writing, the larger the screen and therefore the text size, the better as less eyestrain. Of course, if you travel with a large laptop, you may think it is too bulky. I have used a 17" laptop for years and also when traveling, I don't find it inconvenient. However, as a good compromise, a 15" screen is a good one.

> *If you are going to be writing for many hours, you may want to invest in a large screen to minimize eye strain.*

As you know, there are many brands of computers on the market. Their operating systems are usually either Apple or Microsoft. There are pros and cons to each. Cost may also be a factor in your decision to buy a new one. Ideally, you would purchase a laptop dedicated to your writing and everything associated with your writing such as your writing email address, website, etc. If you are writing as a business, there may be tax advantages. However, that is something to establish and set up with your tax accountant as a minimum and maybe a lawyer.

Of course, writing your book requires a word processing program to be installed on your computer. That program should provide the option of converting your files into both Microsoft if you use Apple and vice versa. It seems that today, publishers prefer the manuscript to meet their format which I have found to be double-spaced, 12 point, Times New Roman font. Of course, your publisher will dictate all that. I prefer writing in point size 14 and then before I send my final manuscript into my publisher, I change to the 12 point size.

It is important that you are familiar with your word processing program so please take the time to learn it. Today's word processing programs allow you to take shortcuts such as in formatting. It will save you time and effort in your writing such as auto spelling, grammar checking. Personally, I prefer to run that as part of my first edit. I want to continue pouring my thoughts into the computer while the creative writing juices are flowing and not be slowed down by red lines under misspelled words, etc. In addition, most of us have had multiple experiences of the predictive software text automatically filling it in with the wrong word. You will be able to correct these errors in editing.

> *When your creative juices are flowing, keep writing and worry about correcting errors in spelling, grammar, and such in your first edit. It is important not to stop for such corrections on your initial writings as writing-stopping-correcting-writing will possibly cause you to lose your train of thoughts, your new idea.*

Some writers will tell you that as they get into the flow of writing, it starts to feel as though someone else is writing and you are just the tool. It may lead you in a direction you had not intended to go but at the same time it is a better direction. Get your thoughts down non-stop as much as possible. When that has happened to me, it feels like an adrenalin rush. There have been times when I've written more than 12 hours straight as I was "pumped" and the story was being written for me, I just typed it. Awesome feeling! You don't try to get there, it just happens. When it does, let it happen, don't question it, don't stop, don't check spelling, grammar. Just type what that inner being is telling you to type.

Depending on what you are writing, you may need a good spreadsheet program and also a program that allows you to create and insert graphics, photographs or illustrations into your book—maybe even a database program. If you are dealing with educational publications, generally they won't send out first proofs until about 60% of the graphics are dropped in.

Both Microsoft and Apple have these programs bundled and compatible with each other. The key is knowing how to quickly and smoothly integrate such spreadsheets and graphics into the manuscript. I've found that when converting my Apple Keynote software to Microsoft's Powerpoint, the format gets messy. If you try to correct it, it will be converted back to Keynote and you're now in a vicious circle. I haven't done so but heard that if you use Microsoft Powerpoint for Apple, this would not happen; however, I have not tried it.

> *One of the most crucial, absolutely crucial things you must do, is constantly create multiple backups of your writings, research, and everything related to your writing. You should be sure to intelligently label them. Remember, dealing with various versions can be difficult. Try to keep it as simple as possible using a good naming convention for your files that you'll still be able to understand a year from now.*

Imagine being months into your writing and your hard drive crashes or your system gets a virus and all your writings are gone. You have to start over again. Would you be able to do that? Would you ever want to? Would that deter you from being a writer, thinking I can't do it? It certainly would be a test of your dedication.

The answer is to constantly backup your writing files. You should back up your files onto various devices such as a USB, an external drive, and some cloud also. Maybe also a read-write CD. At least backup on two other devices. Be paranoid about it. You cannot afford to lose your writings, research material, correspondence with publishers, and other files related to your writing and writing business.

I backup a duplicate copy of all my writing files to a USB drive, an external terabyte hard drive and also have another terabyte drive that I use to do a mirror image backup of my entire system. I normally use a desktop for writing. Once a week I also back up my writing files to my travel laptop. It takes so little time and not doing so may cause you to take several months, if not longer, to rebuild your files.

You may think that is overkill. However, what happens if you are about a year into writing that book, hadn't backed up anything during that time or the last six months and you have a hard drive crash? Think about that and the delays in trying to rebuild your files. Can you ever reclaim those great paragraphs? Would the replacement be as good? You may want to back up your files to some commercial cloud service. I don't see the need when I have it backed up as stated earlier. Besides, you can't hack into an external drives that aren't physically attached to your computer when online. I think for hackers, the cloud files are such a golden nugget and challenge that you'll see more hacks of them over time. Hopefully, your cloud backup provider has good enough security to defend against such things. When they finally admit they were hacked, they may say but no identity theft occurred. Really? How would they really know? Besides, you don't want your information in the hands of others without your permission if for no other reason as the principle of it.

You may even want to periodically print out a copy. I have found over the years, it is still not easy to edit onscreen. I get to a point where I want to edit what I have written thus far, check the flow of the story, and do my grammar and spelling checks. I've found it easier to edit a hardcopy than on screen. I've found that when editing onscreen then printing a hardcopy and editing a hardcopy afterwards, I still find errors I didn't catch when editing onscreen alone. I use my red pen—I use the red pen as it provides contrast to the black text—and edit. I'm always amazed on how many errors of all kinds I find in the first edit. Worse yet, I'm always amazed as to how many issues my editor finds with my "semi-final" manuscript.

If you are already a typist, in other words you can type without looking at the keys, that's great. If you are of the "hunt and peck" type and having to constantly look at the screen, you may want to take a typing course. There are several such software packages that you can purchase and it is money well spent. The benefits include being able to probably type faster and more accurately. When your writing juices are flowing and the words are coming fast and furious, the last thing that you want to have to do is slow down typing, playing catch-up to the words flowing out of your imagination.

SUMMARY

Pick a laptop or desktop that suits your writing environment. Use the word processing program that works best for you but one that can convert between Microsoft's Word and Apple's Pages. Periodically backup your files to multiple devices. How often you backup your writing files depends on how much you can afford to lose. If you don't really know how to type, maybe purchase and practice using a how-to-type software program. As for backing up your files, it's your book so of course your choice. It takes so little time and not doing so may take months, if not longer, to rebuild your files and thus, your book.

CHAPTER 6

ORGANIZING YOUR FILE BASELINE

If you don't organize your book-related files, chaos will reign and you won't be able to easily find what you are looking for cause you added frustration, stress and time. Here's is a suggested way of doing it.

Establish a directory under the name or abbreviated title of your book. For example, if you are writing a book called "My Life", set up a director on your desktop called My Life, ML, ML Project, or some other name that will be the top of the file hierarchy.

Set up subdirectories under that directory called:
- ML-Master Manuscript
- ML-Research
- ML-Notes
- ML-Administration
- ML-Publishing
- ML-Appendices
- ML-Bibliography
- Etc.

Your ML-Master Manuscript, as the title states, is your book's manuscript. Under that directory will be your book's template.

Under your Research sub-directory, establish another sub-sub-directory with the title for each of your chapters. Then when you are doing your research for each chapter, research material goes into a file that is saved under the chapter's sub-sub-directory:

Directory My Life
- ML-Research
- ML-Research Chap 1
- ML-Research Chap x

My preference is to start each sub-directory name in abbreviated form. Using the above, it would be "ML-R-1". May seem complicated but once you start that book using this naming convention, you'll find it rather easy to use. This is just an example. Establish one that works for you.

This is really important since much of your research will probably come from the Internet and that information is perishable. So you must save it for later use, reference, footnoting and such. When doing so, be sure to also write down where you got the information from, such as web site address, date, time, who wrote the information, etc.

This way, when working on a particular book, you click on that directory, then the master book manuscript and start writing. Backup your files and when writing on a different date, change the date to the current one. Then you can choose to delete the previous version or keep the old ones just in case. For example, if your file gets corrupted you only lose a day of writing.

Also, if working on a chapter, you can easily go to that chapter's sub-directory, sub-sub-directory and use that chapter's research material when writing that particular chapter. You should also consider having a separate directory under the master plan for "administrative section". In this section, you will keep all your correspondence with those involved with your book such as your editor, letters to potential publishers, those who give you feedback on your manuscript or book ideas.

While you are writing your book and have an idea for another book or more, or a second edition, you should set up another directory at that time before the idea escapes you. Set up those files as you did with your current book. That way, no matter when you get to the new book, you have already established the file system. When you come across useful information for the other book, you have a place to put it. In doing so, be sure to also identify the source of that information which may be needed later as footnotes or references so you can properly give credit where credit is due and avoid copyright issues. This applies primarily to non-fiction writing, but may also apply to fiction.

> *Some publishers want permissions from sources that you are quoting if the quotes are over 25 words. Some say over 40 words and yet others say 60 words. Discuss this issue with your publisher and use their guidelines. Another way of using other sources is to paraphrase their information but still be sure to footnote the source of that information. It can take 8 to 12 weeks for a permission to be granted. So factor this timeline in.*

There probably will be occasions when you will have research information that is not in digital form. Perhaps a book to use as a reference, clippings from a newspaper, etc. You can always scan the hard copy into digital format and file that way or maybe more convenient would be to keep that hard copy. Another method is to photograph that image and email it to yourself,

A digital filing cabinet should be dedicated to your books and your hard copy file system established identical in format, with titles the same as your digital file system. Basically, your hardcopy files mirror your digital files for each book.

Believe me, having organized files and a project plan allows you to find information quickly and allows you to focus on writing instead of searching for information you have "somewhere". If your book takes maybe a year or more to write, when you are looking a year from now for that research information for your current chapter, you know exactly where it is. To do otherwise means that a year before, you filed that pertinent information somewhere, but will you remember where? Using this system, you won't have to remember because you will know exactly where it is located, e.g. ML-Research-Chapter 21 or ML-R-21.

> *When you come up with an idea for a new book, immediately set up the main directory, using some book title for that possible book, and all directories under it. That way, maybe four years from now when ready to work on that book, you have been collecting research material, maybe writer's notes or parts of that book and now you are ready to write. Use your book template copied to the new book title and add to at least the administrative section as needed.*

SUMMARY

If you have an organized, hierarchy-structured, standard file structure, and file naming convention for each book, you will save time and effort and that process will allow you to focus on writing that book and not waste time looking for this or that file you had stored somewhere on your computer or file drawer, maybe over a year ago.

CHAPTER 7

THE BOOK TEMPLATE

Looking at several published books, you can find a pattern that will help you develop a template for all your books. This generic template can then be used as your format baseline for writing your books.

When you are starting a new book, open the template, make a digital copy, and rename it as the title of your new book.

What is so great about the template is that it gets you to focus on your book's goals, e.g. why you are writing this book, what will be included, etc.

Let's look at a generic book template.

The title page should be the book cover title, sub-title, and your name on the bottom of the page. Your preference or your publisher will decide. Make your main title the largest in one line and a little smaller sub-title line which should be used as the book's descriptive title. Of course, if you have a publisher, they will set it up in accordance with their standards. As part of the book's cover, your name should be as large a font as possible on one line. After all, you spent a lot of time, sweat and tears in writing it, take credit for it.

On that cover will be some graphics or photo that is often descriptive of what your book is about. You can ask your publisher to offer some samples, design one yourself and have your publisher or other graphics designer specialist do one for you. You have the freedom to do the cover as you please, within reason, but in coordination with your publisher. Your publisher may have a contract with an online graphics company who has hundreds of graphics that you can use without a copyright violation. The alternative is to contract with a graphics design firm and buy a design from them that you can use without a copyright violation. If so, be sure they provide you or advertise on their web site that the graphics can be used without violation copyright laws. If you bought it, own the copyright.

> *Publishers have in-house graphic designers and picture teams. The in-house or freelance editor writes a brief or mocks up illustrations, based on the text. Where photographers are concerned, the picture researched will send the editor up to 100 pics for each picture placement. The editor will go through each one on a light box before choosing the pic that fits the textual brief (and budget). If not using a publisher, there are graphics available on web sites—from free to expensive..*

Then next comes the copyright page. Just type copyright page. If you designed or have someone design your cover, give that person credit and state something like: "This cover photograph was taken by B. Elliott Jr. while she was at the Grand Canyon overlooking the Colorado River. Used here by permission". Of course be sure to get her permission in writing. Ask your photographer to email permission for its use to the publisher with you on copy. That correspondence then would be filed in your book's administration sub-directory. That way the publisher is provided assurance that you didn't "forge" her response and send it in to the publisher yourself. Surprisingly, I think that some have done that. In today's world of lawsuits, especially against "deep pockets" entities, publishers are very cautious not to be subject to such lawsuits. Furthermore, when you read your book contract from the publishers, you'll find some legal paragraph or more concerning such things. You can find many examples of cover design attributions in published books. You can use them as examples to write a proper credit.

> *If you did not provide the title cover photograph or drawing, design, you must get permission from the person who provided it (unless of course the publisher provided it), in writing and have that contributor provide the permission, with copy to you, to your publisher whether you self-published the book or not.*

Be paranoid about copyright issues. After all, you wouldn't want someone using your work without your permission, and without giving you credit for your work.

After that page in your book template comes the Dedication, Writer's Quotes if you like that sort of thing, Acknowledgment, Preface, Introduction, Table of Contents.

What's great about that template is it gets you from title to writing the details following a simple format. Let's look at each of these and what to write in each particular section.

Dedication: This section is optional and obviously used to dedicate your book to family and/or others who have supported this book project, or anyone or entity that you wish to include here. It can also be used to dedicate it to all those writers working on their first book. You can say it in any manner you want—within reason of course.

Writer's Quotes: These are optional, useful to quote well-known individuals who talk about whatever it is you are writing about and add their quotes to support your book's topic. You can search online for quote sites such as "writer's quotes". Again, be sure to give credit to the person who you are quoting.

Acknowledgments: This section is also optional but it is used to acknowledge those who supported or helped you with the book writing project. Here you should add some who gave you good advice which you incorporated into the book. Also it's nice to add your book editor and the book publishing project team. It is always a good idea to acknowledge those that gave you the time and space to write. Including your editor is always a good idea.

Preface: This is great as here you can explain why you are writing this book, what you are trying to tell the readers, and your objective in writing this book. Although it too is optional, I think it provides useful information to the reader. It helps you focus and clarify in your own mind why you are writing this book. In other words, you explain why on earth you were crazy enough to take on this project. When writing this book, you probably will have your doubts about the entire project and ask yourself why? If so, refer to your Preface to get back on track or maybe you'll say you can't get there from here and just quit your book writing project.

> *If you decide to quit the project, don't destroy any of your work for at least a year or longer. Deciding to get back to that project will be much easier. If you thought it was worth doing from the beginning, it will probably still be worth it a year or more from now. You may then think, "I could have had my book written and published by now. If only I stuck with it."*

Introduction: This is the opportunity to introduce—explain the topic you are writing about—its importance, and such. It's an optional section. It all depends on you, and what you want to say. It may also include commentary from others about your topic to help legitimize your book's topic. This is generally used for non-fiction. Soliciting experts in the field you are writing about is always a good idea. Don't forget to get their approval in writing to use their information.

If you're writing fiction, you may call this "Prelude", and use it to start your story. Watch any adventure film such as one with James Bond to see what would go in the Prelude section. The beginning of your fiction should grab the reader's interest and keep it.

Table of Contents: This section is required for most books. Its use provides a method to "force" you to establish a flow of things to discuss in your book in some sense of order. Usually used for non-fiction; however, if you use it for fiction, even if deleted later, it will help you focus and have your writing flowing in the direction it should.

When writing your Table of Contents, you will be able to focus on the sequence of events so that your chapters flow in a logical order. You can of course add, edit and delete it as you write. Don't worry about adding page numbers. Your publisher will do that since the final book's format and therefore, page numbers will change.

What I do for personal reference while writing is have my word processing program add page numbers to each page automatically. This obviously comes in handy when finding where you left off writing or editing. It also helps if you have agreed with your publisher to provide a manuscript of a certain number of pages. The manuscript is usually sent to the publisher with double-spaced text. Your publisher will provide you their requirements.

I use the format "x of x pages". I do that so I not only know what page I am writing-editing when I continue the next writing session, but also the total pages so far. This will help you gauge when to write more and when to stop. If your book contract calls for 225-250 pages and you complete the manuscript in 123 pages, your publisher may not approve. On the other hand, if you've written 674 pages, you may have to considerably edit it down. One reason for that is that your book project has a budget. Obviously, printing and shipping a 674 page book, budgeted for a maximum of 250 pages, will exceed the publisher's budget. That will not go well with your publisher. Besides, not many people want to read a 674-page book. Always keep your potential readers in mind when writing your book. Maybe you can save parts of that manuscript for a sequel or second edition?

Appendices: These are used depending on what you want to add to expand your writing examples of something, informative references and other materials that provides more detail. This is usually used in non-fiction books. However, it's your book, the decision is up to your publisher and you.

Index: This section will normally be done by the publisher and is general only used in non-fiction works. However, you may be asked to provide a list of key words on which to base the Index.

Bibliography: This section may or may not be needed. It's used, generally only in non-fiction.

Author's Page: At the end of your book, this provides your biography and includes a photograph of you as an option. I suggest you have one photograph that can be used in all your books and also consider a general biography. The description can be modified as needed depending on the book's topic. For example, if writing fiction, you can say something about being a writer, living in the cabin in the woods or whatever.

If writing non-fiction, your Author's Page should explain your expertise related to the topic you're writing about. If you're writing about traveling the world, include a blurb about your travels over the years to support your expertise in writing a travel book. If you are writing about modern medicine, write about your degrees, where studied, years of experience as a hospital administrator, nurse, researcher or doctor.

The nice thing is that when filling in your template, you can cut and paste your Author's Page from the template and modify as needed.

Back Cover: This includes a short summary of what the book is about, the plot, and be engaging for the reader to buy it. Use character names and situations to whet the reader's appetite. Non-fiction can use bullet points to cover the learning areas that may draw the reader's interest enough to buy the book.

It should also provide something about you. It can also contain some reviews by others to include news media. Of course, that means that you have to give them an unpublished copy to review. Sometimes, you can work this out with your publisher.

If you have friends who know something about the topic you are writing about, maybe you can send them a summary or the manuscript and get them to provide a short comment. Be sure to once again get their permission in writing to use their comments. Their expertise in the area you are writing about is crucial. You may even promise them a free copy of your book when it is published. Again, work that out with your publisher and see if you can get those books for free as part of "book marketing" so it does not count against your personal, free copies. However, you can rest assured that it will count against your royalty as marketing costs are paid and royalties paid only off book sales profits—in most cases at least.

SUMMARY

Using a standard book template offers an efficient and effective way to get started on your book project. Just copy the template file and change the name of the template file to your book title or an abbreviated book title, and begin filling in each section before you get to the main body of your book. It also assists in focusing your thoughts on what is to follow in the main body of your manuscript.

CHAPTER 8

WORKING WITH CO-AUTHORS

There may come a time, maybe with your first book, you decide to have a co-author or co-authors. You may do it because of your co-authors' expertise that will compliment yours, need a ghost writer, or just to share the writing burden.

Whatever your reason, I highly recommend that you establish a process for sharing that book project. In doing so and having your co-author agree, you will avoid some pitfalls that may cause a rift in your relationship, arguments and the like. This is vitally important especially if you are about to enter a contract with a publisher. Regardless of your disagreements, the publisher will probably look at that as a "personal problem" you must work out. The bottom line being the manuscripts due date is probably not going to change.

I once had a co-author who failed to complete his assigned tasks. I ended up writing that part in crisis mode to make the publisher's contract's due date. As stated earlier, in establishing your milestone dates and then doubling them may save you from such a crisis. Actually because of this incident, I decided on doubling some milestone's due dates when writing with others. While at the same time, I have on occasion made my co-author's due dates shorter to be able to meet the true deadline. Remember, once you get your co-author's input, you still have to read it, edit it, and integrate it into your manuscript.

Of course, your co-author should be someone you trust to do their share of the agreed upon work, be competent in writing and as much as possible be compatible with your ideas and writing style. One of my co-authors developed a serious illness and was unable to continue. Remember, that if your co-author(s) does not meet your schedule, it may not be their fault. However, you are still responsible for meeting contractual delivery dates.

Remember, when the book is completed, it should read, as much as possible, as if it came from one author. You may also want to set out to share the writing but each of your writings is clearly being different from one another's on purpose.

Having a co-author is not done out of charity—nor should it be—to help a friend. Remember the old Godfather movie saying about "nothing personal, just business"? Writing a book is a serious endeavor and you should treat it as such from a business point of view.

When writing several books, I've had several co-authors. They were trusted, professional friends who shared similar backgrounds with me and whom I knew were competent writers on the topics that were the subjects of our books.

> *Remember these key words when deciding whether or not to write with a co-author or co-authors:*
>
> - *Trusted to know the genre and topic, and meet deadlines*
> - *Similar or complimentary backgrounds*
> - *Competent writers*

Once you've talked to your potential co-author and reached an agreement on the idea of writing a book together, you must agree on who does what. This is where the book project plan also comes in handy. Using that plan together with your co-author can identify who does what and when. Whether you compress the due dates for their completion is of course up to you.

Also, what is important is that someone, agreed by both authors, is to be the project lead and has control over the book project to include final decisions. This is vitally important because this is not something to become a democratic decision. No, one of you must be the project lead. Yes, of course take advice from your co-author, but if a disagreement ensues, you as the project lead are the final decision-maker. The person with the idea for the book (you) who has decided to write the book with a co-author's vision should be the project lead. That way the book is how you envisioned it to be, as much as possible anyway.

Except for one occasion, I always wanted to be the project leader as I knew what I wanted to write about, what important points to make, and control all aspects of the book project. If any of my co-authors did not consent, I would have written the book without them. Granted, I may have missed some points but better than experiencing all the grief that may have followed if some sort of democratic process were used. Besides, in my case, I was a "semi-retired writer" while they all had full-time jobs. So I had more time to devout to the book writing projects.

The one time I relinquished project lead control was because I was writing two books at one time. Also it gave him, my co-author of previous books, the experience of being a project lead as he went on to do other books without me, including with another co-author who had expertise in an area I did not.

> *Compromises may be needed when working with a co-author(s), but be sure if the book is your idea with your vision, the final result reflects that idea and vision.*

Remember, writing a book is a serious, painstaking, time-consuming endeavor. You will be pouring a lot of blood, sweat and tears into your book. You don't have time for a co-author to miss deadlines without extremely good reason. The excuse that "my dog ate my homework" can never be tolerated. Yes, sometimes delays cannot be helped; however, your co-author should give you as much notice as possible if a delay will occur and when their input will be received on reschedule.

You should have an agreement at the beginning of your writing project that your co-author agrees to provide you immediate warning of any delay. Your co-author should not wait until the deadline is due to tell you that the date cannot be met.

If there is to be a delay, don't forget to look at your project plan and modify the dates for completion. You must also look at the dates of work to be done based on the delay. It may have a trickle -down effect or it may not. Either way, you should update your project plan.

If you and your co-author are on contract with a publisher, you will have a manuscript delivery date. If not met, there may be serious contractual consequences, from a reputation, contract and financial standpoint. Remember, that if your co-author turns out to be unreliable, you may have to consider dropping that person as your co-author. If so, you must consider the ramifications and do so before offering another person that co-author position. Actions to be taken also depends on whether or not you both are on contract for the delivery date of the manuscript. It is vitally important to keep your publisher apprised of all developments that impact the delivery of you manuscript.

If your co-author requests payment from you in advance, don't do it. You should never pay someone to be your co-author. Furthermore, they should also bear half the costs associated with the book project or you recoup that as part of your share of the book royalties. Keep in mind that you may never sell enough books to recoup that money. Consider whether or not you want to absorb that loss of funds.

SUMMARY

Having a co-author has some advantages and disadvantages. Before you decide to have a co-author, consider the ramifications as objectively as possible. Maybe make a list of pros and cons on a piece of paper. Then make your decision to offer someone that opportunity then discuss it with your potential co-author. Be prepared to discuss in detail what you had in mind, who does what and when. Show your potential co-author you project plan, modify as necessary. Writing a book is difficult enough. You don't need the added burdens of an unreliable co-author. Do your homework.

CHAPTER 9

BOOK RESEARCH

Whether you are writing a book of fiction or non-fiction, chances are very good that you will have to do some research. You may wonder why do research if you are writing a fictional story? Your book of fiction may require a little to a great deal of research. After all, even fiction, with few exceptions, should be believable.

A fantasy book taking place in a make-believe realm or a sci-fi book of life in another world, should have some believability. In other words, it could happen, it could exist.

When do you begin doing research for your book? Research should begin as soon as you have that idea for your book and you have made up your mind that you will soon begin writing it. As mentioned earlier, once you have an idea for a book, come up with a title, use your book template to provide the details, at least the outline of the book. The Preface, and if you use an Introduction section, those sections enable you to put down in writing what your book is going to be about.

Before you go any further, visit book-related websites such as Amazon and other online book sellers, maybe also your local library, at least the library online. Put in the working title of your book and also the book's topic. See if there are any books out there with that title. Also, see if there are any books out there that cover the topic you want to write about. If so, how different is your book from those books already published?

This is very important because if your book title is rather close to others out there, you should come up with a convincing argument as to why you should keep your book title. Titles may not be copyrighted but same or similar titles to your upcoming book may cause increased competition. Furthermore, if you plan to use another's title and piggyback on their success, that may be illegal. Such things must be discussed with your publisher. If your topic has been covered by previous author(s), why is yours important, different? If using a publishing company (not a self-publishing company), you'll have to explain that to them.

If you can't come up with some very valid reasons, even though the book is near and dear to you, you should consider putting it away for another time. Maybe your competitor will not be putting out another edition or the competitor's book is outdated, you still have a chance to get your book published. If a competitive book has already been published and it is popular, consider not writing that very similar book or use a variated title.

Remember, books are copyrighted by the publisher or the author. If your book uses ideas from another, beware of copyright infringements. Always give credit to your sources.

Now that you have done that initial research and found no true competitors, it's time to start the next phase of researching. There are several ways to do that and of course it's up to you to choose how you want to do it.

You can do your research for the entire book before writing the book, do both at the same time, or only doing research as needed. All approaches have pros and cons. You can even do a combination of all of them. Let's assume your book will take you a year or more to write. Consider that when you are near the end of writing your book that the information previously gathered is outdated. Therefore, to be a current book, your research should be as current as possible. Remember that from the time you submit your final manuscript to the publisher, it may be three to six months or even longer before your book is published.

I found the method that works best for me is as follows:
1. Come up with a book idea
2. A working book title
3. Search online for competitors
4. If found, decide to proceed or put in limbo
5. If no competitors found, charge ahead

6. Write a project plan
7. Establish your specific book template
8. Write the Dedication
9. Write the Preface
10. Write the Introduction
11. Write the book's Table of Contents
12. Set up the book's Directory and all sub-directories using the chapter titles as naming conventions for each file
13. Identify primary online research sites
14. Identify non-digital research entities, e.g. periodic magazines, conferences to attend, people to interview, etc.
15. Establish a research process.

I then start writing my book in accordance with the book's project plan. I'll do daily research by accessing my online and hardcopy targeted research sites for any info that may be valuable for the specific chapter I am working on. When I find relevant information, I copy that information into a file and place that file into the particular sub-directory book chapter that I have created.

When doing your research, be sure to also list in that file the source of your information. This is extremely important because although generally you can quote 40 words of what someone has written as previously noted (this varies by publishers as some may say 20-25 words, others 60 words), you must give them credit for that information you are quoting. This is vitally important and can not be stressed enough. You must obey copyright laws just as you would want someone to do if they used your original information. In addition, you should footnote or reference in your book the source of that information. Whether the footnote is at the end of that page, end of that chapter or the end of the book, it is up to you if you self-publish but even then, the publisher will have a style guide, which will decide the book's format, to include where to place footnotes, i.e. end of the book or bottom of the page where it is cited.

You can always try to obtain copyrighter's permission to use the information. In the past, I've tried on several occasions to do that from other than my publisher who owned copyright authority for the books I want to quote from, and I never heard back from them or they say no. Although one author I contacted said yes once we negotiated a fee for its use. Needless to say, this time I said no. It seems to me, they would agree whether you are a publisher or author since they would be getting free marketing through the visibility of their book in my book.

> *If you want to quote someone or some publication and need to obtain written permission from the copyright holder, it is best to ask for that permission as soon as possible because it may take several months before you get a reply.*

So, you are writing along and think you could use some detailed information about a certain matter. You first go to your research sub-directory for the chapter and see if that information is there. If so, great. If it's not, you go to your research sites and documents, and find it. If it's not there and is important for your book, you can leave a note in the midst of that chapter to get that information at a later date (and just highlight it in yellow so it gets your attention on first edit). That later date can be when the chapter is finished or when the book is done in first draft and you are beginning your second draft. If you are in the midst of a great writing session, best to leave a note where you want to consider that information in that chapter and keep writing. Remember, when writing that first draft, it is crucial to get as much of your book out of your head and onto that blank page as soon as possible.

It is also important that your research information be as current as possible. Therefore, even if you found the material you were looking for in your sub-directory, it may be outdated.

What if you can't find it? Maybe that is a good thing as you may have just come up with a unique idea and be the first to look at the idea in a new way.

You have now established your writing schedule and your research schedule or at least the research process that you will be doing such as daily research site sweeps, or research on an as-needed basis while you are writing.

SUMMARY

Book research is a vital process to be used when writing your book, especially when writing non-fiction. You should always be looking for relative information, filing it in the appropriate chapter's research file. Using the research information for each chapter as you write it.

I generally do six edits before my manuscript goes to my editor or publisher's editor. Sometimes, I do more than six. It all depends on how satisfied I am with my manuscript. During each edit and re-write, I continue to look for current information (when writing non-fiction books) and incorporate it into the applicable chapter.

When I complete my book but before I send it to my publisher, I do one final sweep online for current information. After all, your book should be as current as possible. It would be a shame to miss some vital new information because you were too lazy to do that final research.

Remember, online information is temporary, perishable. So when you find it, grab it as it may be gone the next day.

CHAPTER 10

THE BEGINNING

Always keep your audience in mind. Write to them and, if you are writing on a topic you also enjoy reading about, put yourself as objectively as possible in the reader's position.

In your project plan, you wrote a simple objective but it was probably a rather general objective. Now, you should consider writing the book's specific objective.

If you are writing non-fiction, your objective will be different from writing fiction. In writing non-fiction, you're writing a formal book where you will have a table of contents which may include your book in sections and under each section, chapters. You will need formal references set to publisher's instructions for authors that will probably be on your publisher's web site. You should also consider a section page listing all the chapters in that section, and the chapters' titles.

Also consider the format for each chapter. For example, have an "Introduction" for each chapter that explains what the chapter is about. Also consider a "Summary" at the end of each chapter. As the old saying goes: Tell them what you are going to tell them, tell them and then tell them what you told them[1].

In your non-fiction book, you probably want the reader to learn new ideas, becoming aware of certain information. For example, this book's objective may be to provide the reader with an introduction to writing by

---

[1] There are various versions of this statement that was developed over the years. The originator is unknown by this author.

providing a process, an administrative plan to effectively and efficiently be organized to write your book and have it published.

If you are going to write fiction, let's say a novel, then having a table of contents is optional, generally depending on you and/or your publisher. It is assumed that you will have chapters and chapter titles.

Look at books you have read and/or others and find a style that you like. Unless the style is very unique and may be copyrighted, you can probably use it. If you look at many books of fiction by various publishers and writers and see the same pattern, that format that you want to use should be just fine.

Why do I go into such detail about such things? It is because you do not want to plagiarize just as you don't want your work to be plagiarized.

More thoughts on copyright: If you want to use someone else's work to reference that will require permission of the copyright holder, just look at their copyright page. You'll find it is the author or the publisher that holds the rights. You must contact them in writing and get their expressed, written permission. The few times I wanted to do this, I never got a reply. So don't count on anyone giving you permission. If they do, pay attention to what they have specifically approved.

The times I had been contacted by a publisher or author to use my non-fiction copyrighted book information, I stipulated that my book be acknowledged in the Acknowledgment section of their book and that I get a free copy of the book where my work was quoted. Just something to think about. Charging the requester for use of your information is always a possibility but I never do that. Call it professional courtesy. I may also stipulate that I can use their information in one of my books and our written agreement would include that permission. Why not as free advertising of their book in yours and vice versa?

When writing any work of fiction, I like to use my book template and use a Table of Contents (ToC). When the book is completed, I may or may not keep that ToC. However, when I am writing the first part of the book, what I call the Administration section that consists of Title Page, Preface, Acknowledgment, Introduction, and ToC and back page, I use the ToC to lay out my story.

Using the ToC for a work of fiction allows you to summarize the events of your story and you can look at that to develop where you start and where you finish—-the beginning, middle and the end.

As stated earlier, if you watch movies related to the genre in which you decide to write your book, you will note that something immediately happens to catch the viewer's attention. Then the movie goes back in time to start the story.

This gets viewers interested and when writing your novel, you must catch the reader's interest in the first few pages. The first paragraph is best.

For example, you are in a bookstore, library, or online book website. You find the genre you want and perhaps scan for authors you are interested in, or maybe a title catches your eye. You open the book and read the administrative section or go right go the first page of the narrative.

The first page is where the story begins. It should catch the reader's attention and intrigue you enough to want to read the book. A Prelude section describes an event like a murder that takes place and the rest of the book explains the murder, what led up to that murder, and the capturing of the killer.

> *Be sure your book grabs the readers' attention on the first page. If not, the reader will think, no thanks, too boring, and put your book back on the shelf or if online, select another title, especially for works of fiction.*

You should always figure out how your novel, textbook, or such, will flow. You will probably find it is so much easier to write the beginning of the book and the ending. The more difficult part of writing your book, especially fiction, is how you get from the beginning through the middle to the end, while keeping the reader's attention.

This of course is the crucial part. You must have the story evolve in a logical and entertaining way. One thing you don't want to do is to weave a story and near to the end you have one person explain everything in a long explanation that goes on for pages upon pages.

SUMMARY

A good novel gets the reader hooked in the beginning, keeps the reader hooked throughout the story, and comes up with some periodic surprises, some characters the reader will like and some the reader will hate. This should all start at the beginning of your book of fiction. That is why it is important and probably gives you an advantage if you also read many books, especially in the genre of your book.

CHAPTER 11

THE END

In writing a non-fiction book, you have a Table of Contents (ToC) and at least the first draft of your book will be based on that. Having a ToC is great as it lays out your flow process.

When writing fiction, I recommend you still use a ToC as this provides you with a direction, an overview flow to your story. You can always delete the ToC when your book of fiction is completed.

Consider drafting a detailed flow chart from the ToC. Basically, you flow out the main milestones of the story. An outline form may also be useful. I use a whiteboard to do that as I can stand back and see the story unfold. You can add decision points and have your characters decide to go one direction or another.

The difficulty in writing fiction is keeping the reader interested from beginning to end, building up the action, tension, and such throughout with perhaps a surprise ending. Build these type of things into your flowchart or outline. If you don't have any of these tensions or major surprises, you can see where they are lacking and add them.

> *It may be easier to write the beginning of "once upon a time" and the ending of "they all lived happily ever after". The real difficulty is getting from the beginning to the end while keeping the reader wanting to continue reading, not wanting to stop.*

You may find that as you write, your story takes you in another direction and you end up with an alternate ending. There's nothing wrong with that of course, but make sure it is a logical conclusion. For example, you write a murder mystery and in the end you decide that the murderer should not be identified. Think about how your readers will feel reading such a book. They'll probably be disappointed, maybe even angry? Probably. You may think it is an interesting ending but maybe just speaking for myself, I wouldn't read another book by such an author. I want a good read that comes to a surprising but logical conclusion. I do not want to read one that doesn't. Then again, I don't watch a TV series that goes on and on. If you do and enjoy it, maybe such an ending would be ok for you. You'd be willing to wait for a sequel or two? However, that does not mean you can't write in such a way as to not only come to a logical conclusion, but also hints of a sequel.

Your ending should leave your reader wanting more from you. Perhaps stories that involve the same main character(s); like the Harry Potter series by J. K. Rowling, and the Robert Langdon series by Dan Brown, just to name two.

You can and should try to surprise your readers by having a surprise ending, but when looking back throughout your book, it should make sense. There should be that logical link connecting the beginning to the end. And that is done through the "middle". Then again, there are those who identify who the killer is upfront, and you wonder why it is that person. The book then leads to the culprit. The detailed outline and flowchart can provide that roadmap.

Keep in mind that after you edit and rewrite and edit again, rewrite again, you should set the manuscript aside for a week or so. Then go back and read it once again. You may find that it sounds rather good and you may question yourself. Did I really write it? On the other hand, you may read it and think it is terrible. If so, you'll have a lot of work to do. With all that said, you can only fine tune it so many times. You'll reach a time when you just need to stop. If there is much more to add, consider a sequel, or a second edition instead.

In writing non-fiction, you may want to consider adding a "Final Comments" section that wraps up all that you have said. If you do so, keep it rather brief. If fiction, you can also have a "Conclusion" section. It may be come after the murder is solved. Your conclusion section by whatever name, says they lived happily ever after in so many words.

SUMMARY

The ending of your fiction book should culminate in a logical and maybe surprising ending. Your ending should not be a long narrative explaining all that happened in your story. That path to the logical conclusion should have been woven throughout your story. By not doing so, you are not doing the story justice. You may do so out of lack of story writing experience or laziness. Regardless, don't do it.

Using a ToC as a basis for creating a detailed outline or a flowchart may help you visualize your story and its flow, and find gaps in the story.

CHAPTER 12

THE MIDDLE

When reading non-fiction, you generally find there is no real middle but an even flow linking one chapter to another in a logical sequence. There are no surprise endings and there may be a logical conclusion reached by presenting all the information from the beginning to the end.

In fiction however, the middle is the fun of intrigue, twists and turns, maybe romance, surprises—but they must make sense. Each writer has their way of getting from the beginning to the end and the more you write fiction in a specific genre, the more you can develop your magic formula that works for you.

So, you've done your administrative section, including your Dedication, Acknowledgment, working ToC. Now you do your exciting Prelude or first chapter to set the tone for the rest of the book's story. Your action Prelude to hold the reader's interest through at least that part, is set. Now, the real story begins to evolve over the next XXX-plus pages.

This is where a ToC, detailed outline and flowchart are so useful. It will be your guide to get you from beginning to end. You should develop the ToC in sufficient depth so that it will provide much of the middle narrative. For example, you may have a chase scene which by its vary nature is an exciting part of the middle. The idea is to use the ToC as your story's outline and with each re-write of it, you add another lower level of detail until you reach the point when you have written sufficient amount of detail to then expand each item that ends up connecting the beginning to the end in a logical way. You may also use an outline format that builds on the ToC.

If writing non-fiction, it may be based on a lecture, or speech that you gave. If so, it is much easier to write that book based on your speech, or lecture which can be developed through the use of a slide show using presentation software. That being the case, your ToC may be the slideshow headers. Each slide or section of slides may be your chapters. If so, just write your first draft as if you were giving that lecture. Type as you talk it.

All good word processing or related software programs has an outline format. When writing your book, start the outline with your chapter titles and then continue to write in bullet format the main points in each chapter of your book. In doing so, you can easily see the flow of your book. In fiction, this is helpful, maybe more so than non-fiction. That's because you can evolve your story by stating the main points that are to be the heart of that chapter. The more levels down in your outline, you should eventually reach a point were you are about at chapter paragraph level. If so, then just expand your bullets into sentences. I know it sounds easier than it actually is but over time you should find this technique is a valuable tool.

SUMMARY

When writing non-fiction, there probably is not a middle but just an in-depth discussion of the book's topic. However, when writing fiction, the middle of your story is the heart of it. How you get from the beginning to the end while holding the readers' interest throughout is where your writing talent and imagination will be tested the most. That is the most difficult part of writing any fictional story.

CHAPTER 13

EDITING AND DEALING WITH AN EDITOR

I mentioned that over the years I've averaged six edits before the manuscript went for final edit to my editor. Over time, you'll find a suitable number of edits that works for you.

I like to have my book as complete as possible before it goes to my editor. Maybe it's writer's pride. Maybe it's not wanting to get a bunch of questions back on this or that in the manuscript when I thought it was complete. Also, a simple grammar and spelling check when you are about ready to read one final time and send to your editor, will make your editor happy.

There are several types of editors[2]:
- Editor assigned to you by your publisher when under contract with a publisher who are paid by the publisher.
- A professional editor who you pay to edit your manuscript. Generally, when you are paying for editorial service, it is because you will be self-publishing your book.

If you pay for a professional editor, it is often based on the amount of hours that are needed to be done. So, another good reason for you to do as many edits as needed so that the time and thus the fee required to be paid is as small as possible.

---

[2] The next chapter will discuss the various types of editors in more detail.

There are many freelance editors who you can contact. If so, be sure to check their reputation and editing credentials, fees. You can also have your trusted family and friends read it first. However, unless they are professional editors, I highly recommend you do not trust them as the editor of your book. To me it's like trusting someone to operate on your brain after they saw it done in a television documentary.

However, since you have been deeply involved in writings, editing, re-writing your book for probably a year or more, you might want to consider their help. They can help you find typos, spacing issues, and also point out what they don't understand that you may want to consider re-wording.

Editing fees vary by editors. I believe $20 an hour is reasonable. Some may charge a base fee to start and some may also charge by the number of pages edited. Don't forget, as the saying goes, you get what you pay for and when you go cheap you often get cheap.

One first time writer I know paid her friend who was supposedly an editor. I am not sure of that editor's background but I received a copy of that book and found errors, including simple typos. The main issue as I see it is that my friend was in such a hurry to get published that she sacrificed quality. Don't.

> *When paying an editor by the hour, it behooves you to provide the best manuscript possible as it will take less time to edit and save you money.*

Now that your book is done and ready for a publisher (non-self-publishing books), it will be assigned to a team to include an editor. It seems that these days, editing is outsourced to another company in order for the publisher to save money.

The problem I've run into is that there seems to be on more than one occasion that the assigned editor does not understand what I said and what I meant by what I said. On one occasion, the editor tried to put my book into an academic, sort of textbook format and sent me so many requests for this or that information.

I explained I was not writing an academic book, textbook but more of a how-to book for professionals. Finally, I got to the point that I asked my publisher to assign me another editor. I've also found some editors were very good and I had little difficulty with them.

There is more to editing than just checking spelling and grammar. There is also format, flow of your narrative, identifying gaps in your manuscript where somethings don't properly flow into one another and so much more.

If you are writing with a co-author, they also should be involved in the final edit before you give it to a professional editor. Hopefully, that will help cut down the amount of errors in the manuscript.

> *There comes a time when after spending a year or more on your manuscript that you can't see the forest for the trees so to speak. This has been made clear to me on occasion. I thought my manuscript was error-free. Unfortunately, my editor's red-inked pen seemed to cover more of each page than my black-inked-text.*

When I work with a co-author, we sit down together and one of us begins reading the manuscript and the other one makes agreed-upon changes in real time—of course on the manuscript's computer file. After a while, we switch so that one of us doesn't get tired of reading and the other of typing changes. This process goes a long way in eliminating errors. It varies by length of the manuscript but on average it takes us 2-3 days because we are reading the entire manuscript during that time, discussing changes, adding new material, etc.

> *Although a woman who has had a baby will disagree with me when equating the pain of childbirth to the "birth" of a book—and have—I look at writing a book like being pregnant and having a baby. You get that publishing contract and the joy that comes with that just like a woman becoming pregnant. Then as you work on that book day-after-day for more than a year, it's like the pregnant woman about to have a baby. After 8+ months, she is miserable and just wants to give birth—at least that is what I have been told. As a writer working on a book for whatever length of time, you reach a point where you just get sick of the topic and just want to get it done. I've experienced that with each of my books—maybe it's just me.*

Like the birth of that baby, your manuscript, turned into a book is like that baby. You get your published copies of the book, hold it in your hands and your baby has been born. After I get my copies of the book, I use some for marketing and I put one on the shelf never to look at it again. I just wanted to be done with it. By that time, I'm already involved in a new book.

As I complete the editing and re-writing of this book, I've already started another book. By that I mean, I have started a new project plan, installed the book template and completed what I call the administrative section: Cover, Table of Contents, Preface, Dedication, Acknowledgment, Prelude, etc.

To get your book through publication, it will take a team effort of editor, managing acquisition editor, graphic designers and others. Your professional editor is a key member of that team and sometimes knows more about how to best present your manuscript in book form than you do. Yes, it is a team effort, at the same time, it is your story, your manuscript and if changes that are wanted by the editor significantly changes your manuscript, and you believe not for the better, you should listen but the final decision should be yours.

A word of caution though: always be open to the advice of experts such as your editor and other professional members of the publishing team. If they call your "baby" ugly, think about it. Maybe it is and you should take their advice.

SUMMARY

It is not mandatory but if you want your published book to be as error-free as possible, a professional editor is required. If you sign a book contract with a publisher, they will provide an editor for you to work with. These editors are paid for by the publishing house so no cost is incurred by you, the writer.

If you self-publish your book, you will have to pay your self-publishing company for an editor or pay for an independent editor. If you pay for an independent one, you should check out their costs, reputation, how long they have been in business, examples of books they have edited and maybe talk to the editor's clients. However, the editor may not want to share their customer's identity. There may be good reasons for that and not necessarily be trying to hide negative information.

CHAPTER 14

FROM THE EDITOR'S DESK

Anonymous

Writing for a readership is daunting. Whether you write on paper or onscreen, there is always that initial terror of *The Blank Page.*

That blank page will stare you in the eyes until you confront it. It can make you feel either inferior or elated. It may not be your choice. You have to go with the flow. Embrace it either way.

You chose this blank page. So do something about it.

Before we even believed in ourselves, we are worried that our readership might reject us immediately. Some will. Some won't. Trust in yourself.

> *A note to authors: You begin writing with that blank page, as depicted on the book's cover, staring at you. Your blank page can be your friend or barrier to a successful book. If you consider it your barrier, stop and find another career or hobby. You should enjoy that blank page as you can write on it whatever you want; empty your story onto it.*

The Boring Stuff

An editor either works by being employed within a publishing company, a corporation, or freelances from home/self-managed facility.

We are basically "critical readers" who refine the text for the writer we are working with. There are many types of editors, and include:
- Acquisitions Editor
- Film Editor
- Script Editor
- Media Design Editor
- Desk Editor
- Many, many other editors.

The word 'Editor' is okay to stay in as it's part of a proper noun. There are no full points at the end of each bullet point unless they were full sentences. Just one at the end to denote the severance of the information—and the sigh of relief for the reader.

> *Your editor is like the referee or umpire of a sporting event. They are experts on the rules—in this case grammar—and are the enforcer when editing a writer's manuscript. You can argue with them but best to listen to them and follow their lead.*

The bullets are introduced by a colon. This denotes 'the following', stuff to come. So, you don't have to write...

... as you can see by the following: I digress, I'm not supposed to be teaching English or how to edit... so let's crack on.

So What Does an Editor Do?

It's all about language, grammar, and stuff. The giving of accurate information, research, and a dose of procrastination (information management).

Many freelancers work from home at all hours of day and night depending how many books we are editing and their due dates back to our clients—the writers. The reason for editing is three-fold to include protection against:
- Plagiarism

- Copyright infringement
- Author's reputation.

The third point here is to enable your author's credibility.

An in-house or freelance editor must adhere to the in-house style-guide. Some are only 17 pages long to remember, others can be 370 pages long (these are usually the top medical style guides). It is a constant learning and referencing point curve to deal with.

The Global Editors

The profit margins are shrinking. So as is the case of most businesses, the publishers look for cutting costs, increasing profits. One way they do this is by outsourcing parts of their publishing process to entities in other countries with cheaper labor force costs. That includes outsourcing the editing process. For example, I trained editors in India for four years for a major publisher. I live in the U.K., but I edit for writers in other countries, such as Dr. Kovacich in the U.S.

Today's readership is global and therefore, editors must be able to edit for a global readership and keep that in mind when editing for clients. A writer must consider that and depending on the topic of the book being written, must consider the ability of the editor to understand that global or specific country audience. For example, I use the Roget's Thesaurus as my guide. It is used in Britain by editors; however, most of it can be applied globally.

We all have different editing roles. One of the contributions to our roles is to support and supply our writers and fellow staff with a good coherent bond. Whomever we are, togetherness makes for success.

Symbiosis: Writer and editor are in sort of a symbiosis relationship. This is how Editors and Authors try to meet the brief. One generally gets annoyed with the other, and the feeling is reciprocated. But we get there in the end.

Final Thoughts

Editors and writers both write prolifically. Both sets of people edit down, write up, rewrite. We work together on the best presentation and readability for the reader; the audience.

In academia, it's paramount that accuracy and legality comes first. In fiction, it's a very different story. In a non-academic publication, it is important to keep the author's voice. As rules no longer apply, but the author's character should shine through.

So, although it may seem easier to edit a work of fiction – it isn't.

SUMMARY

Writers and editors must work as a team for the writer to be successful. The editor is the writer's best friend and worst enemy. It's a marriage of two professionals with the same objective and that is have published a professionally, well-written book free of errors.

Both should be experts in the rules of the language they are writing in; however, that is a must for the editor who "cleans-up" the manuscripts of the writer.

The writer must be able to take constructive criticism from the editor—and others in the publishing process. It is always best to listen to your editor. They may not always be right but they are seldom wrong.

CHAPTER 15

PUBLISHING HOUSES

The publishing business continues to evolve and now more than ever it is becoming a difficult business in which to make substantial profits. Discounted book sellers, like amazon.com, ebook business, self-publishing houses all have had major impacts on this business.

> *According to bowker.com, more than one million books were self-published in 2018. Depending on your book's genre, they represent the competition for readers.*

In the old days, writers write, mail hard copy, typewritten manuscripts to various publishers and sit around waiting to be contacted or when you called them it was more of "we'll call you, don't call us". So, what do you do? Sit around waiting for a publisher or publishers to get back to you? Do you send to one publisher at a time, or many publishers at once? You're at their mercy—at least you once were. Now, due to advances in technology, that is not the case with the advent of e-books and self-publishing firms.

At the same time, as a writer, you are in a world of massive competition to get your book accepted by a publisher. However, due to the ease of publication through multiple choices of how to publish your book, you also have more flexibility. Once accepted by a publisher, the competition to have the reading public's visibility to your book is also difficult.

> *According to statitca.com, in 2018, the unit sales of printed books in the U.S. was about 695 million. This number represents your potential market of readers.*

For one thing, people don't seem to read as much as before when we now have so many other forms of recreation to choose from. This seems to be especially true for the younger generations. In addition, when they read, they're now reading ebooks. For publishers, the competition has never been greater or the profits smaller.

> *Some publishers will not accept unsolicited manuscripts. Furthermore, they won't even send you a rejection notice. Search various publishers' websites for their policy on manuscript submissions.*

Technology has been a friend to the publishing business but also an adversary. Sort of a Yin-Yang thing. It has made publishing more efficient and yet has caused a massive increase in publishers—those that are self-publishing houses. Also, because of technology, the number of new books published each year seems to increase on an exponential basis.

According to statista.com:
- Annual book sales in U.S.: 675 million, revenue of $26.23 billion
- Ebook sales of 163 million; penetration in book sales rate is 26.1%
- 67% of U.S. population read at least one printed book in a year.

According to Wikipedia, in 2013 in U.S., 304,912 books were published. According to publishers weekly, "Unit sales of print books rose 3.3% in 2016 over the previous year, making it the third-straight year of print growth."

The statistics available per year seem to lag making current statistics more difficult to find. However, the point is, you will have a great deal of competition for publishers and readers' attention. Self-publishing houses are the exception because you have the funds, they have the publishing capabilities.

My experience with publishers and self-publishers when it comes to the time from submitting my book proposal, through contract signature to publication were very different. I've used three well-known publishers for my books. This has been my experiences with them for my non-fiction books:

- Complete their online form for my book proposal
- Wait 1-3 months for a reply
- If yes, I sign a contract
- I usually want a year to complete the manuscript and submit it
- They review it, assign an editor who gets back to me with questions, comments, requests for re-write, clarifications, and such
- I answer all their questions, re-write as needed
- They usually send the manuscript back for final approval
- They send the book covers for final approval often based on what I wanted the covers to look like
- The book is sent to publication
- I receive the book.

That process from book proposal submission to book publication may take over one to two years. I usually don't use a self-publishing house unless my manuscript is complete or nearly complete. There are exceptions. For example, if a self-publishing house that you have identified for having your book published is having an online sale where you save 20% or more if you order now, you may want to take advantage of that sale. On the other hand, you can wait until your manuscript is done and wait for another sale. Your book, so your decision of course.

When dealing with a self-publishing house, I contact them, review and sign their contract with a manuscript ready to go. They review it, then send out their form with questions. I answer their questions, submit what I want for book covers (front and back), and generally have the book in my hands in about 90-120 days. The self-publishing process is faster even when considering I have a manuscript ready to go. Yes, the time is cut down since I have a manuscript ready to submit; however, the self-publishing process is faster by months. I think the reason being is that they are less bureaucratic, more streamlined.

> *Royalties are paid at the same time each year and I usually have to wait six months to a year after publication for that first royalty check. The royalties of course depend on profits after subtraction of marketing costs, copies I requested, advances, publication costs if not self-publishing. It all depends on their royalty payment cycle.*

The advent of ebooks and increased popularity of audio books, make the publishing business more interesting and more challenging than ever before. Furthermore, the opportunity to receive advances on your book seems to be dwindling—except maybe for very successful authors..

It is a time of greater competition, smaller margins, and more and more driven by technology. At the same time, it makes it more convenient for writers. For example:

- I live in the U.S.
- Co-author lived in UK
- Publisher was in Germany
- Contract signed electronically
- We were paid out of Netherlands office
- Royalties wired directly to our separate accounts.

This was all done through emails and Internet communications. Can you imagine if it was done many years ago?

- We would write, snail mail our various manuscript parts to each other
- Edit
- Then one of us would integrate it, type and retype
- Publisher would mail the contract for us to sign and mail back
- Editor would mail the manuscript to us
- We would address the issues, etc. and mail it back.

How much time do you think that process would take? Obviously many more months just in mail time alone and also consider the costs of internationally mailing 225-plus pages of your manuscript between yourself, co-author, and publisher.

SUMMARY

The writing business, and publishing business as a whole, is rapidly changing and continues to evolve. As a writer, you should keep up-to-date as to these changes because you will be impacted in both positive and negative ways. Know your writing—publishing environment so that you can take advantage of these changes and at the same time, avoid their pitfalls.

CHAPTER 16

FINDING A PUBLISHING HOUSE

The Internet has made life much easier for writers. Not only in doing your research for your book, but also when looking for publishers. One of the first things to decide on is whether you want to use a publishing house that will probably own your book's copyright, and pay you a royalty on an annual or semi-annual basis.

It seems that today, with today's book contracts, you have little room for negotiating the percent of your royalty and advances. However, you should have some room to negotiate a manuscript delivery date. It seems more likely than not, especially as a first-time writer of a book, you'll have to settle for what they give you. Advances on your book, unless you're famous or infamous, have pretty much disappeared. Royalties also on average have seemed to decline. Publishing is a business and of course publishers want to make a profit and/or improve their reputation globally (citations-driven publishing in academia). Therefore, using their business model, they'll estimate their costs and their expected book sales; therefore, their profit margin.

Once you sign that contract, you must deliver the manuscript on or before it's due and in the format they require. One thing to keep in mind is if you do not meet your delivery deadline, you may be responsible for paying the salaries of your publishing team if there isn't any other work for them. Why is that? The work is scheduled based on receiving the manuscript on time. Therefore, the editor, the person working on your book cover, et al. are ready to work on their scheduled project dates. If idol because of your delay, you may be liable for their salary in consideration for your royalties. Check your contract carefully. This may be an extreme;

however, I suggest you find out in advance as to the penalties for not delivering according to your contract. That's why, especially as a first-time book author, it is always a good idea to have your manuscript done at least in first draft if not completed before contacting a publisher. In this way, there isn't the pressure of a looming delivery date at the time your book is far from completed. I know you want to get your book into print as soon as possible but err on the side of caution.

> *Writing a book is work but it should also be fun. Don't ruin the experience by trying to get a contract and have a non-realistic manuscript due date when you're not ready.*

The method you use to find a publisher is of course up to you. One method is to look for the publishers listed in the books you enjoy reading and who also publish books in the genre you are writing. There are also books of publishers with details as to what they publish, and their submission criteria. Check your local library or online for such books. The business is constantly changing so I suggest you get the information for free online or from a book at the local library.

Another way to research your publisher/audience is to buy a copy of Writers' and Artists' yearbook. This is updated every year and makes for good bedtime reading. It talks in genres, has expert advice, and is exciting to the point that it encourages you to go for it.

> *Never be without marker pens, highlighters and sticky notes when reading this book. Use it as a resource book, a work book. Use its a a reference and don't be afraid to scribble all over it.*

Using the online method is to do an Internet search using your criteria such as publishers that specialize in science fiction, or murder mysteries. Something to consider is that you may be writing a book that competes with their authors in the same genre. If so, would they ever consider a contract with you, a first-time book writer? Then again, maybe they would to expand their "stable of writers". However, first you must get them to read your book proposal or manuscript. That in itself is a major hurdle. These days, unsolicited manuscripts come pouring into publishers and more likely than not it seems rejected out of hand as they use that old adage: "Don't call me, I'll call you." Your unsolicited manuscript may end up on the "slush pile" with a rejection note to boot.

> *I've heard from one acquisition manager that he received a manuscript in a box (pre-email days). When he opened it, confetti fell out all over his desk and floor. The writer apparently thought it was cute and get his attention. It did. He immediately trashed it. The lesson is of course don't try "cutesy" ways of getting a publisher's attention. Then again of course I could be wrong. Your manuscript, your risk. This applies to emailing attempts as attention grabbers also.*

Read the interviews of some well-known authors as they explain the hundreds of rejection notices they received before someone took a chance on them. After knowing about those, you may want to give up or just the opposite—continue to persevere! I hope you want to persevere since you worked so very hard for such a long period of time to become a published writer.

Once you've identified a group of publishers who meet your criteria of accepting manuscripts from new writers and who publish books in your manuscript's genre, you should go to their website. They may have on it a book proposal form for you to fill out. In doing so, read carefully what they require and give them what they require and only what they ask for. These days, more than ever, hardcopies have gone the way of carbon paper. Generally, submission of your manuscript must be sent digitally. My experience has been a requirement to send in Times New Roman, double-spaced, text size 12 and filling in their form. Some require you to submit your manuscript using Microsoft Word. However, my current publisher has accepted my manuscripts in Apple Pages. Some also now accept other software formats.

> *If you are using your favorite software but will submit your manuscript using another software application, use caution as sometimes it may not provide a 1-1 conversion with the result being format or other types of errors.*

Let's look at an example of the steps in publishing your book through "7 Steps to Publishing" with CRC Press:

Step 1: Write your book proposal

Step 2: Submit your book proposal

Step 3: Obtain approval of your book proposal

Step 4: Sign the contract for your book

Step 5: Prepare your book manuscript

Step 6: Submit your book manuscript

Step 7: Production.

Such proposal forms are also great to print off before you even start your book. This is because it focuses your attention on what needs to be kept in mind as you write your book. You should also consider them among your major milestones in your project plan. Also, the information you must provide helps you focus on your manuscript and some of the information can be used in your manuscript's template administrative section.

Think about your book from a publisher's point of view. Publishers are interested in profits and reputation of course and you must convince them that your book is worthy of their attention, and they can make money off of your book sales. Also, keep in mind that your proposal or manuscript will be reviewed by an "acquisition manager"—sometimes called an acquisition editor. That person wants to ensure as much as possible that the book they agree to publish will be profitable. They will probably present your proposal to a committee that meets once a month to go over all proposals.

If they have a string of non-profitable books, their jobs may be in jeopardy. Therefore, they'll probably decide no before they decide yes—unless of course you are one of the famous or infamous authors.

You can go online to your targeted publisher(s) and see what information they require. Let's look at some common requirements that I have found when dealing with four different publishers. As you read through these bullets, write your responses to these questions as the publisher will read them, and what that publisher is looking for—answers that will convince them to publish your book and they will be able to make a profit in doing so; as well of course as pay you royalties. Information usually required by the publishers include:

- What is the title of your book?
- Who are you?
- Contact information
- Qualifications on the topic you are writing—especially needed for non-fiction
- What is the book about?
- What is the target audience?
- Marketability of the book
- Table of Contents
- Sample chapter(s)—helps them determine if you can write
- Recommend reviewers—non-fiction for sure
- Is it a textbook?
- What course topic?
- How many estimated charts, photos, etc.
- Estimated number of pages
- Specific countries targeted
- Written in what language?

SUMMARY

From a publisher's point-of-view you can see that you must convince them to commit funds and staff to your book project. They will only do that if you convince them that it is a topic of interest to readers, you're qualified to write it, and it will sell. In other words, if you are the publisher, would you publish your book? Be sure to be as objective as possible in making this decision so you don't waste your time.

CHAPTER 17

FINDING A SELF-PUBLISHING HOUSE

If you are going to self-publish your book, you still have to conform to their standards. The major difference is when going to a publisher, they incur all the costs. When going to a self-publishing firm, you incur all the costs.

Because of technology, many self-publishing firms have sprung up and you may find an umbrella company having several self-publishing firms. The difficulty is finding a "legitimate" one that will publish your book and do so in a professional way. Also, you want to be sure that the quality of your book is as good as that of the popular publishing houses. In other words, quality paper and print, pages don't fall out of the book. You want your book to look and feel as if done by a large, professional publishing firm that has been in the business for quite a while. In other words, they do a professional job and continue to survive the competition.

You want your book to be one you can be proud to have written and self-published. You don't want to have a book published for the sake of having a book published. Take pride in your work. You must do your research and do it well. In today's market, where thousands of writers want their books published, many self-publishing firms have sprung up. You may find that some are more reliable than others.

There are online sites that evaluate self-publishing firms and provide commentary on them. Again, be cautious. Do any of these sites have a vested interest? or recommend one or more firms over others? Are the recommended firms all under one corporation? Just as it seems many glowing online product reviews are done by the product company, the same may apply to self-publishing firms.

> *Be very cautious because you will be using your money. Therefore, be concerned with frauds and other scams.*

Basically, you are going to be paying for specific services. If photos and graphics are above a certain free number, they'll cost extra. Editing? Extra. Marketing? Definitely extra.

> *Since I like to self-publish many of my books, such as this one, you may think that I have vetted this self-publisher and I have. However, I do not endorse any publishers, recommend any publishers. The ones that work for me may not work for you. In addition, a self-publishing firm may be bought out, management changed, and there are various other reasons why what works for me may not work for you.*

In the past year, I have been inundated by self-publishing firms by phone and emails. It appears that they check online for self-published books and try to "make you an offer you can't refuse". Think about it. Some person, often with a foreign accent in a foreign country, calls or texts you, offers to have their publishing company re-publish and/or market you book, for example $2000, more or less. When you look up their publishing company online, you may or may not find them. If you do, it may only have been in business for a year or less. That in itself is not bad as all businesses start from nothing and in fact, they may offer special deals to get started. However, do they have the experience to publish a professional product and/or have connections to properly market your book. Be careful in your drive to publication. Be sure you verify the credibility and publishing ability of your potential self-publisher.

Ask them to provide information relative to:
- How long have they been in business?

- Where is their headquarters?
- Where are their other offices?
- Is their firm a privately-owned or a publicly traded company? (Publicly traded companies have to meet certain government requirements whereas privately-held firms do not always have the same public scrutiny).
- How many authors do they currently support?
- What are their names?
- What services does the publisher provide?
- What is the cost of each service?
- Where are their books listed for sale?
- What guarantees do they offer?
- Why should you choose them?
- What separates them from the competition?
- Who are their competitors?
- What are the royalty splits?
- How often will you get a royalty?
- How will they market your book?
- Who will edit your book?
- What is their experience in editing books in your genre?
- Where are their editors located?
- Where is the printing house located?
- Will the book be in the Library of Congress?
- Will they submit and receive ISBN numbers for my book as part of the cost of publishing my book?
- Who will own the copyright for your book?
- If not you, why not since you're paying for its publication?
- What are the distribution channels for your book?

You can probably think of more questions to ask. They may not be forthcoming with all the information. The more evasive they are, the more you should ask more detailed questions.

Once you are satisfied with the responses of all the publishers you have contacted, you must decide which publisher to do business with. Use the tried and true investigative questions of who, what, where, when, why and how to be as sure as possible you'll be getting what you will pay for.

You may also want to check with the state's attorney general's office to see if they are under investigation. Also check with the Better Business Bureau for complaints against them.

SUMMARY

Self-publishing houses have been growing in number. You will be spending your own money so be sure that you will be getting your money's worth of support. Search online for self-publishing houses, look at their services and the cost of those service.

Also do your due diligence by asking questions that will give you confidence that the firm you choose will provide a professional publication of your book. If you use their marketing services, be sure they have the connections to get your book wide-spread visibility to potential buyers. Don't be lulled into a deal by their flattery. Put your ego aside and be objective. After all, it's your money.

CHAPTER 18

NEGOTIATING A BOOK CONTRACT

Congratulations! You have found a publisher that is willing to consider your manuscript. You'll probably be assigned an acquisition manager to be your project lead, focal point, whatever their title. This person will be your "best friend" with whom you will be teamed with to publish your book. They'll probably be your main point of contact for your publisher; however, it will be a team effort. You, an acquisition manager, editor, graphic designer, printer, marketing staff, and others.

They'll probably send you a standard contract. As a new book writer, you may want to immediately sign, maybe even without reading it in detail. Obvious word of advice: Don't!

It is vitally important to thoroughly read the contract, maybe even give it to your lawyer for review and comments. While reading, make a list of questions that you can ask the publisher for contract clarification, or have your lawyer do it. Be sure you understand all of it as it will be legally binding on you. Some of the possible negotiating points are the delivery date of the manuscript to the publisher in the format defined in the contract. Another possible point of negotiation is an advance. As previously mentioned, nowadays, your chance as a first-time writer of getting an advance is, as they say: "slim to none". Furthermore, your royalty negotiating will probably be limited with much depending on their costs of publishing your book using their formula, considering number of pages, graphics, photos, illustrations, and other related expenses or maybe their standard royalty percentage for new writers.

After all that is figured out and in concert with your publisher, you should provide input to the following:

- book size
- paperback
- hardcopy
- e-book
- book cover color
- book cover text color
- book cover graphics, artwork
- back of book text, design
- retail prices for each type.

You'll also want to know:

- discounted price for copies you purchase
- preferred published book spacing (1, 1.2, 1.5)
- unsold books after a while can be returned to the publisher and that may impact on your royalties
- how often are royalties paid.

Remember, the suspense date. Caution, it may be upon you before you know it. Remember, we discussed your book writing project plan? It is a great vehicle to pace yourself. If your project plan extends your writing past one year, negotiate your due date accordingly. If they are reluctant, having that project plan provides good justification and shows that you have thoroughly thought out this project. A copy to them may help with your due date negotiations.

As a first time book writer, it may be better to first write your book and then look for a publisher as they will want to know how soon your book will be ready for submission[3]. I don't know who said it but recall a saying: "God laughs while you plan" And I think John Lennon said, "Life happens while you're making other plans".

---

[3] Throughout this book, I reiterate certain matters as they are extremely important and deserve some redundancy in explanations.

> *I know that you are probably excited about writing your book and getting it published. However, there may be unforeseen events that delay your writing or you may not be able to finish your book. For your first book, consider writing it and then be prepared to submit the manuscript within a month. Less stress and pressure that way.*

Hopefully, you won't be like me when I wrote my first book under contract to a publisher. I negotiated a delivery of the manuscript one year from contract signature date. So, I thought, one year is a long time and really didn't start on it right away. However, when I realized the manuscript was due in three weeks, I ended up writing sometimes almost non-stop for 20-plus hours. I vowed to never do that again. That was the first lesson-learned: develop a book writing project plan and pace yourself starting the day of contract signing. Ironically, it was my best selling book to date and in its third edition. Luckily, the fact that it was based on a lecture I had given 7-8 times made it easier to write.

After your book is published and hopefully a great success, further book negotiations with that same publisher will be familiar to you and you may even be able to get an advance or higher percentage of royalties since you'll have a proven track record with them—assuming your book makes a profit. If not, prepare for rejections from that same publisher. Each book proposal is considered on its own merit but after your first book, your history with that publisher is also considered.

The book price is set by your publisher; however, if using a self-publishing firm, you have some say-so in setting the price. I generally go by their recommendation as they know the market better than I do. The economics of it all probably means if a high price, better royalties. However, maybe less books may be sold. Whereas, a lower price may mean more books are sold and actually more royalties established although the royalty percent is lower.

Another key point: When they read your manuscript, they may not like it and reject its publication. Check your contract carefully for such a clause.

SUMMARY

When you receive a book contract, be sure to completely read it in detail at least once or more. Maybe even discuss it with your lawyer, to include any possible negotiating points such as due date, advances, royalties and marketing. Once you sign that contract, you are legally bound to provide a manuscript as described in the contract before or ahead of time. If you submit the manuscript late without their approval, you may incur additional financial penalties.

CHAPTER 19

MARKETING YOUR BOOK

Once you've completed your book, and had it published, how do you get people to notice it? If you are using a regular publishing house, they will use their marketing channels to make the book visible to potential readers. Your book project plan should have a detailed section identifying your marketing plan strategy as a subset. That plan should have laid out the various tools to use to market the book.

If you use a self-publishing house, they should make the book available to book sellers such as Amazon and Barnes&Noble, library outlets, and the like. However, some may have a policy of not doing more to market your book unless you are willing to pay more for their "marketing expertise and process".

However, it is also up to you to market your book regardless of what type of publisher and what specific publisher you use. How do you get your book in front of potential readers? Let's look at the several ways you can do that.

You can pay to have the book advertised in newspapers, magazines and such. You may find it is cheaper to do it yourself or you may find doing it through your publisher to be cheaper and more effective. The business terms "efficient" and "effective" come to mind. In other words, which method gets you more for your money. For example, in what newspaper should you advertise? You should choose the one that is most popular and has a book section. It's not cheap but it may maximize your book's visibility. The bigger the advertisement, the more visibility, but also the more the cost.

If you have written a non-fiction book, find a conference that includes your related topic and even volunteer to give a related lecture using your book to build your presentation. Then of course your intro unashamedly says this lecture is based on your book, entitled…. At the end of the lecture, show the cover of the book and say available at selected bookstores and online sites, or have a box of them to sell with signage. However, if you bring some of the books to your lecture to sell, you must consider how many to purchase, albeit discounted, from your publisher. If you sell only a few, what do you do with the rest that you already purchased?

Another method is that before you start the lecture, is to work out a deal with your publisher to have your book available at a discount with a code that the attendees can use when ordering your book through your publisher's web site. Your publisher should like that as it not only will help increase the visibility and potential sales of your book but also provide the publisher with increased visibility. Furthermore, they are able to cut out the "middle man" for commissions. However, there is a downside. Discounted sales means less profits and less profits to the publisher means less royalties to you. Another method is to give free lectures at related associations and libraries.

You should also target journals, and magazines for submitting articles based on excerpts from your book. They may not pay you but the point is to make your book visible to as many people as possible.

Another method is to hire a marketing agent. Let them use their connections to help sell your book. Invariably, this may require that you give talks on your book's topic at bookstores and then do a book signing afterwards. The embarrassing part of that is what if only a few or no one shows up?

You may have or want to consider establishing a website in which you can consider writing as a business and also sell other services based on your expertise. Of course, best to check with your accountant and/or lawyer for advice. I don't have a website, although my publisher set up a website for one of my other books that they published. I enjoy the pure art of writing and concentrate on that. I leave it to the publishers and others to deal with the book's other things such as marketing. So, try any method you can think of to get your book in front of potential buyers. Of course, if you are not writing for a living, and any royalties are considered "fun money", then marketing may not be high on your list.

If you are writing as a "hobby" or just for the joy of writing, it may not matter whether your book sells or not. You write off your costs when using writing as a business and so your loss of an unsuccessful book may not be that bad. Of course, much depends on your finances. See your accountant and/or lawyer for all that.

> *Using a 3:1 approach to market your book:*
>
> - *Use a lecture as a basis for writing your book and write articles from that book and lecture*
> - *Use your book as a basis for articles and lectures*
> - *Write articles that can be used for lectures and chapters in your book.*

When dealing with the newspaper, journal, magazine concerning publishing excerpts from your book, be sure to maintain the copyright so you can use that information as you please. If your book is copyrighted by the publisher, be sure to get their permission in writing. They will probably agree since you are marketing the book and they also get profits from any sales that may be a result from your 3:1 approach.

Remember also that this is the age of social media and is it being used more frequently to market books and replacing the traditional methods of advertising in magazines, newspapers. Some may use podcasts and blogs. For some, t may be used to replace book signings in person, etc. Something to consider in your marketing strategy. Of course, that is something that is also worth discussing with your publisher.

SUMMARY

Marketing your book is the joint responsibility of you and your publisher. In most circumstances, when using a self-publisher, you will have to pay for it. You can market your book through book signings, giving lectures and writing magazine, and journal articles based on your book. Also consider establishing your own web site, blog, use social media to market your book(s).

CHAPTER 20

TAX IMPLICATIONS

There are tax advantages to being a writer as a business. Of course, each situation is different for each writer. There are implications based on book-writing income, other incomes, tax category, and which country or state you live in.

I am no way an expert in such matters and leave that all to my tax accountant. Besides, tax laws change over time and you must use the current tax laws. One word of advice, never lie to the tax person. No matter how much you think you will save by cheating, it is never worth it when they find out and possibly take your assets and in worse case scenario charge you with a criminal offense, found guilty, and incarcerate you.

I've included this chapter so that you are aware that being a legitimate writer as a business does have advantages you may want to consider. I advise that before you do write as a business, consult your tax accountant, your lawyer or some professional who is experienced in such matters. Laws are often changing so rely on your tax accountant and/or lawyer to provide you with advice related to those issues.

If you write as a business, your book writing project plan should also consider keeping track of all expenses related to your book, receipts from purchases of writing related tools and supplies such as ink cartridges, new computers, printers, paper, and such. If you do so and that equipment is used solely for writing it is easier than figuring out what percent is used for writing your book and take that percent as a tax write-off. Again remember that tax laws change, your income may change and thus, impacts your taxable income.

There are other possible write-offs such as the footprint of your writing space in your office, utilities used as a percentage of your writing time. You may find that such tracking is not worth the small advantages from a tax standpoint.

SUMMARY

Writing as a business may have tax advantages depending on what country and state you live in. Seek advice from a professional tax expert and determine in detail what can be used as tax deductions and income related to your writing.

CHAPTER 21

FINAL THOUGHTS

A Writer's Life

Many want to be a writer,
But few really try, or
Have the talent to succeed.
No matter, write for yourself.
It's a lonely profession,
Even with a co-author.
It can be frustrating,
A natural high—or low.
Choose wisely: write or not.

-Gerald L. Kovacich

As you may have gathered after reading this book, there are many aspects of writing that go beyond just sitting down at a computer, using a word processor and writing a book. If you are serious about writing, having a book writing project plan is very useful to focus you on writing that book and where you can also measure your progress. Develop a book writing process that will work for you. I hope I have given you at least a useful baseline for such a process and some things to think about before you even begin to write your book.

I've heard from publishers, wanna-be writers, and others who mostly want to be writers and never follow through. Yes, it is a lonely profession for those who are extroverts. It is a great profession for those who are introverts. It gives you an excuse to be alone and left alone. If you are somewhere in the middle, it may work too.

Those whom have no idea of the effort it takes to write a book, let alone a successful book, think you may have an idea, may come up with a title, and may just write it. Oh if only it was that simple.

> *Writing should be shear joy. Once you get the bug, don't go to the doctors. Let that marvelous bug stay with you. Enjoy the ride! - Sandy Nichol*

If after reading this book, you decide not to try writing your book, I hope I didn't scare you off. I encourage you to at least develop a book writing project plan. Then like someone once said: "How do you eat an elephant? A bite at a time." If you don't take the challenge, I hope a few years from now you don't look back and regret your decision, thinking you could have had it done already.

If you decide to take on your book project, I wish you the best of luck and much success. Remember, even the most successful writers started with their first book. There is no reason why you can't be a successful writer. Maybe "fortune and glory" awaits. However, if not but you enjoy writing, keep it up. Just enjoy the experience. My editor-in-chief, Sandy Nichol, and I wish all new writers success in their quest to have their first book published.

ABOUT THE AUTHOR

Gerald L. Kovacich has always been a writer beginning with love letters to girlfriends growing up to getting paid $1 for each love letter he wrote for his U.S. Air Force friends. He has progressed over the years from writing articles, internationally and nationally consulting, lecturing and writing books on cyber security and information warfare. He has also lectured on international travels. Now, he enjoys writing non-fiction books of poetry, short stories, essays and other works of fiction.

When he is not writing, he is traveling the world, enjoying life's experiences, meditating, exercising, and just hanging out thinking of writing his next book of fiction or non-fiction. He also spends time with his editor and her husband in England eating Cheetos and drinking wine; watching zombie and "B" rated movies; while trying to get her cats away from his new manuscript she is editing. When asked why he writes so much, he says, "Because it's fun!"

OTHER BOOKS BY DR. KOVACICH AND CO-AUTHORS

Fiction

- *Poems of Life: Thoughts of Human Experiences* (AuthorHouse; 2012; ISBN: 978-1-4772-9634-9; 978-1-4772-9633-2; 978-1-4772-9632-5) Kovacich.
- *Essence of Her: Collected Poems* (AuthorHouse; 2015; ISBN: 978-1-5049-0368-4; 978-1-5049-0369-1) Kovacich.
- *Ramblings of an Old Man* (AuthorHouse; 2015; ISBN: 978-1-5049-0909-9; 978-1-5049-0943-3) Kovacich.
- *The Book of Waking Dreams: Stories of the Dream Man* (AuthorHouse; 2015; ISBN: 978-1-5049-0370-7; 978-1-5049-0371-4) Kovacich.

Non-Fiction

- *The Alzheimer's Plan: Caring for a Family Member* (AuthorHouse; 2019, ISBN: 978-1-7283-1822-6 (sc), 928-1-7283-1821-9 (hc), 978-1-7283-1820-2 (e)) Kovacich/Anensen-McNealley.
- *Information Systems Security Officer's Guide: Establishing and Managing an Information Protection Program* (Elsevier; 1998; ISBN 0-7506-9896-9; Czech translation available) Kovacich.
- *Information Systems Security Officer's Guide: Establishing and Managing an Information Protection Program* (Second Edition; Elsevier; 2003; ISBN 0-7506-7656-6) Kovacich.

- ***Information Systems Security Officer's Guide: Establishing and Managing an Information Protection Program*** (Third Edition; Elsevier; 2016; ISBN 978-0-12-802190-3) Kovacich.
- ***High-Technology Crime Investigator's Handbook: Working in the Global Information Environment*** (First Edition; Elsevier; 2000, ISBN 13: 978-0-7506-7086-9; 10: 0-7506-7086-X). Kovacich/Boni.
- ***High-Technology Crime Investigator's Handbook: Establishing and Managing A High-Technology Crime Prevention Program*** (Second Edition; Elsevier; 2006; ISBN 13: 978-0-7506-7929-9; 10: 0-7506-7929-8). Kovacich/Jones.
- ***High-Technology Crime Investigation*** (2009; Chinese Translation) Kovacich/Jones.
- ***The Manager's Handbook for Corporate Security: Establishing and Managing a Successful Assets Protection Program*** (First Edition, Elsevier; 2003; ISBN: 0-7506-7487-3) Kovacich/Halibozek.
- ***The Manager's Handbook for Corporate Security: Establishing and Managing a Successful Assets Protection Program Instructor's Manual***; (Elsevier; 2005; ISBN: 13: 978-0-750-67038-1; 10: 0-750-67938-7) Kovacich/Halibozek.
- ***The Manager's Handbook for Corporate Security: Establishing and Managing a Successful Assets Protection Program*** (Second Edition, Elsevier; 2017; ISBN: 978-0-12-804604-3) Kovacich/Halibozek.
- ***I-Way Robbery: Crime on the Internet*** (Elsevier; 1999; ISBN 0-7506-7029-0). Kovacich/Boni.
- ***I-Way Robbery: Crime on the Internet*** (2000; Japanese Translation; (ISBN: 4-89346-698-4) Kovacich/Boni.
- ***Netspionage: The Global Threat to Information*** (Elsevier; 2000; ISBN: 0-7506-7257-9) Kovacich/Boni.
- ***Information Assurance: Surviving in the Information Environment*** (First Edition, Springer-Verlag; 2001; ISBN: 1-85233-326-X) Kovacich/Blyth.
- ***Information Assurance: Security in the Information Environment*** (Second Edition); (Springer-Verlag; 2006; ISBN: 10: 1-84628-266-7; 13: 978-1-84628-266-9) Kovacich/Blyth
- ***Global Information Warfare: How Businesses, Governments and Others Achieve Global Objectives and Attain a Competitive Advantage***

(Auerbach/CRC Press; 2002; ISBN 0-8493-1114-4) Kovacich/Jones/Luzwick.

- ***Global Information Warfare: The New Digital Battlefield*** (Second Edition, Auerbach/CRC Press; 2016; ISBN-13: 978-1-4987-0325-3) Kovacich/Jones.
- ***The Corporate Security Professional's Handbook on Terrorism*** (Elsevier; 2008; ISBN: 978-0-7506-8257-2) Kovacich/Halibozek.
- ***Mergers and Acquisitions Security: Corporate Restructuring and Security Management*** (Elsevier; 2005; ISBN: 0-7506-7805-4) Kovacich/Halibozek.
- ***Fighting Fraud: How to Establish and Manage an Anti-Fraud Program*** (Elsevier; 2008; ISBN: 978-0-12-370868-7) Kovacich.
- ***Fighting Fraud*** (2010; Russian Translation; Ernst & Young; ISBN: 978-5-903271-31-30) Kovacich.
- ***Security Metrics Management: How to Manage the Costs of an Assets Protection Program*** (First Edition, Elsevier, 2006; ISBN: 13-978-0-7506-7899-5; 100-7506-7899-2) Kovacich/Halibozek.
- ***Security Metrics Management: How to Manage the Costs of an Assets Protection Program*** (Second Edition, Elsevier; 2017; ISBN: 978-0-12-804453-7) Kovacich/Halibozek.

www.ingramcontent.com/pod-product-compliance
Lightning Source LLC
Chambersburg PA
CBHW031133250726
48655CB00002B/650